HOUGHTON MIFFLIN HARCOURT

Comprehensive Language and Literacy Guide

Consultant
Irene C. Fountas

Grade 2

Copyright © 2011 by Houghton Mifflin Harcourt Publishing Company

All rights reserved. No part of this work may be reproduced or transmitted in any form or by any means, electronic or mechanical, including photocopying or recording, or by any information storage and retrieval system, without the prior written permission of the copyright owner unless such copying is expressly permitted by federal copyright law. Requests for permission to make copies of any part of the work should be addressed to Houghton Mifflin Harcourt Publishing Company, Attn: Contracts, Copyrights, and Licensing, 9400 South Park Center Loop, Orlando, Florida 32819.

Printed in the U.S.A.

ISBN 13: 978-0-547-36880-1
ISBN 10: 0-547-36880-1

3 4 5 6 7 8 9 10   0877   18 17 16 15 14 13 12 11 10

> If you have received these materials as examination copies free of charge, Houghton Mifflin Harcourt Publishing Company retains title to the materials and they may not be resold. Resale of examination copies is strictly prohibited.

> Possession of this publication in print format does not entitle users to convert this publication, or any portion of it, into electronic format.

Comprehensive Language and Literacy Guide

A Readers' Workshop Approach

Introduction: What Are Effective Instructional Practices in Literacy? 1
- Whole-Group Teaching 2
- Small-Group Teaching 4
- Independent Literacy Work 6

Planning for Comprehensive Language and Literacy Instruction 8

Whole-Group Lessons 39
- Interactive Read-Aloud/Shared Reading
- Reading Minilessons

Teaching Genre 101

Appendix 112
- Leveled Readers Database 112
- Literature Discussion: Suggested Trade Book Titles 124
- Professional Bibliography 129

Introduction

What Are Effective Instructional Practices in Literacy?

Your goal in literacy teaching is to bring each child from where he is to as far as you can take him in a school year, with the clear goal of helping each student develop the competencies of proficiency at the level. Proficient readers and writers not only think deeply and critically about texts but also develop a love of reading. The roots of lifelong literacy begin with a rich foundation in the elementary school.

The **Comprehensive Language and Literacy Guide** provides a structure for organizing your literacy teaching, linking understandings across the language and literacy framework, and building a strong foundation of reading strategies and skills. On the pages that follow, you will find an overview of how to use this guide along with your *Journeys* materials in three different instructional contexts: Whole-Group Teaching, Small-Group Teaching, and Independent Literacy Work.

WHOLE GROUP
Interactive Read-Aloud/Shared Reading
(heterogeneous)

WHOLE GROUP
Reading Minilesson
(heterogeneous)

SMALL GROUP
Guided Reading
(temporary homogeneous)

SMALL GROUP
Literature Discussion
(heterogeneous)

INDEPENDENT
Independent Reading,
Independent Literacy Work

Whole-Group Teaching

👤 TEACHER'S ROLE

- Engage children in thinking deeply about texts.
- Provide a learning environment in which children feel comfortable sharing their thinking with each other.
- Prepare explicit lessons that are tailored to children's needs.
- Provide a model of phrased, fluent reading in interactive read-aloud.
- Prompt children with comments and questions at planned stopping points to promote active thinking in interactive read-aloud/shared reading.
- Provide explicit teaching of critical literacy concepts in reading minilessons.
- Expose children to a wide variety of genres, authors, and topics.
- Monitor children's understanding to plan for future lessons.

👥 CHILD'S ROLE

- Listen actively.
- Share ideas and opinions with others.
- Make connections to other readings and to own experiences.
- Ask genuine questions and build on the ideas of others.
- Demonstrate understanding of critical literacy concepts.

Whole-group lessons lay the foundation for the day's instruction and give children the tools they will need to apply what they have learned in other contexts, including small-group instruction and independent literacy work.

PLANNING FOR COMPREHENSIVE LANGUAGE & LITERACY INSTRUCTION
For each lesson, or week of instruction, select from the menu of items shown on the Suggested Weekly Focus page, or use all of them.

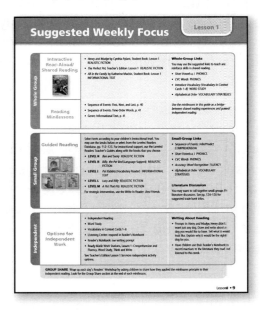

◀ Plan whole-group teaching using the menu of options provided.

WHOLE-GROUP LESSONS The Whole-Group Lessons are related lesson sequences you may want to use across a week. At the core of each lesson is a *Journeys* literature selection, chosen to highlight a certain aspect of reading that is important for children to learn and apply in various contexts.

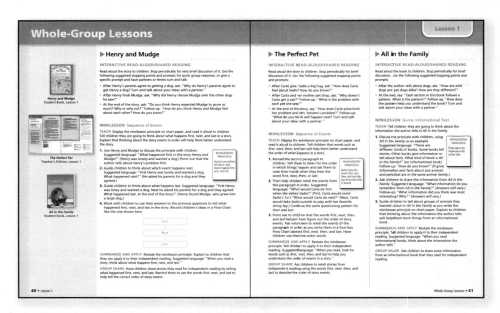

▲ Interactive Read-Aloud/Shared Reading and Reading Minilessons build and expand children's understandings, using a *Journeys* literature selection.

2 • Whole-Group Teaching

JOURNEYS RESOURCES FOR WHOLE-GROUP TEACHING
- Student Book
- Teacher's Edition Read-Alouds

Parts of Whole-Group Lessons

1 **Interactive Read-Aloud/Shared Reading** sets the stage for the day's focus and provides a common foundation of experience for children at various levels of reading proficiency (Fountas and Pinnell, 2006). In Interactive Read-Aloud/Shared Reading, you read aloud to children and encourage discussion of the reading through questions and prompts at planned stopping points in the text. Reading aloud to children in this context will help them appreciate literature, and they benefit from your modeling of how to think about ideas in the text as well as from the thinking of their peers. In addition, Interactive Read-Aloud/Shared Reading

- serves as a model of fluent, expressive, phrased reading.
- provides a context for getting children to think actively about what they read.
- allows children to hear a variety of perspectives and interpretations.
- is the common text used as an example in the Reading Minilesson.

2 The **Reading Minilesson** is the second part of your lesson. The minilesson is focused instruction about a specific topic or skill, called the Minilesson Principle (Fountas and Pinnell, 2001). Using this principle, you help children think like effective, independent readers. The literature selection from Interactive Read-Aloud/Shared Reading context is used as the example to demonstrate the principle.

TEACHING GENRE Genre instruction is a powerful tool for helping children develop the competencies of effective readers and writers. The questions and teaching points in this section can be used over and over across the year as children encounter different genres and increasingly difficult texts within a particular genre.

▲ Integrate meaningful genre instruction into your whole-group teaching. Select from the teaching points, questions, and materials provided.

Whole-Group Teaching • 3

Small-Group Teaching

 TEACHER'S ROLE

GUIDED READING
- Form groups based on children's instructional levels.
- Establish routines and meeting times.
- Select and introduce the book.
- Monitor children's reading through the use of running records and specific questioning.
- Record observations.

LITERATURE DISCUSSION
- Form groups based on children's reading preferences.
- Demonstrate routines for effective discussion.
- Facilitate discussions, and redirect student talk as needed.
- Summarize children's ideas and engage them in self-evaluation of their contributions.

CHILD'S ROLE

GUIDED READING
- Apply skills learned during whole-group instruction.
- Share ideas.
- Make connections to other readings and to own experiences.
- Ask questions.
- Support thinking with evidence from the text.

LITERATURE DISCUSSION
- Choose a book.
- Prepare by reading and thinking about the text.
- Listen politely and respectfully to others.
- Share opinions and raise questions.

Small-group lessons are the individualized sessions in which you help children develop as readers based on their needs, challenges, and sometimes their preferences.

GUIDED READING In guided reading lessons, you use *Journeys* Leveled Readers to work with small groups of children who will benefit from teaching at a particular instructional level. You select the text and guide the readers by supporting their ability to use a variety of reading strategies (Fountas and Pinnell, 1996, 2001). Guided reading groups are flexible and should change as a result of your observations of your students' growth.

In this guide, whole-group lessons provide the foundation for small-group instruction. Skills introduced in whole group can be developed and expanded according to children's needs in a smaller group with the appropriate level text. On the Suggested Weekly Focus pages, Leveled Readers that connect to the whole-group experience are suggested, though you may need to select from the complete Leveled Readers Database (pp. 112–123) to match your children's instructional levels.

PLANNING AND RESOURCES Using the small-group resources in this guide, along with the Leveled Readers and the Leveled Readers Teacher's Guides, you can plan for and teach lessons that will develop the competencies of your particular students.

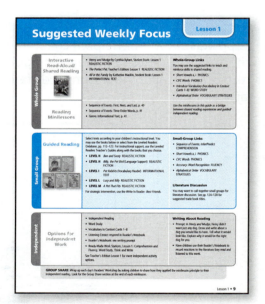

◀ Plan small-group teaching by considering the options on the Suggested Weekly Focus or in the complete Leveled Readers Database.

◀ *Journeys* Leveled Readers Select Leveled Readers according to the instructional levels of your students.

4 • Small-Group Teaching

JOURNEYS RESOURCES FOR SMALL-GROUP TEACHING
- Leveled Readers
- Leveled Readers Teacher's Guides

  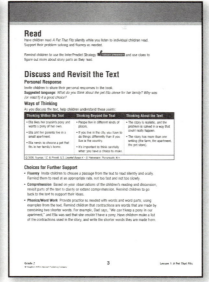 

▲ **JOURNEYS Leveled Readers Teacher's Guides**
Support children as they read Leveled Readers at their instructional level. Use lessons in the Leveled Readers Teacher's Guides to promote the following:

- Thinking Within the Text
- Thinking Beyond the Text
- Thinking About the Text
- Writing About Reading
- English Language Development
- Phrased, Fluent Reading

LITERATURE DISCUSSION Literature discussion brings together a small group of children of varying abilities but who may have a common interest—a topic, a genre, or author. Children have selected the same book to read and have prepared to discuss it. In this collaborative group, you facilitate discussion of the book and encourage children to share their thinking and to build upon each other's ideas as they gain a deeper understanding of the text (Fountas and Pinnell, 2001).

The members of literature discussion groups will change as children select different titles or topics. One advantage of Literature Discussion is that all readers can benefit from each other's thinking, regardless of their instructional level.

It is important to guide children in selecting books. Introducing a range of books through book talks is one way of sharing several options for reading. Encourage children to sample a book, or read a short segment, to determine whether it is too easy or too difficult before they make a final selection. If a text choice is hard for the student to read, someone can read the text to him or her at school or at home.

A wealth of trade books can be used for engaging literature discussions. The Suggested Trade Book Titles on pp. 124–128 are appropriate for Grade 2 students, and a wide variety of genres, authors, and topics are represented. Select books from this list and make them available for children, or use books in your library.

Independent Literacy Work

👤 TEACHER'S ROLE
- Establish classroom routines for independent work time.
- Set expectations for what children should accomplish.
- Confer with individual children to discuss books or sample oral reading.

👥 CHILD'S ROLE
- Follow established classroom routines.
- Engage thoughtfully in reading and writing tasks.
- Take responsibility for assignments, and demonstrate progress.

Independent literacy work includes meaningful and productive activities for children to do while you work with small groups.

It is important that your students engage in meaningful, productive activities when you are working with other children (Fountas and Pinnell, 1996). This is an opportunity for your students to build mileage as readers, to develop good independent work skills, to collaborate with others, and to work at their own pace. The Suggested Weekly Focus for each lesson provides options for independent work that expand on the week's instruction.

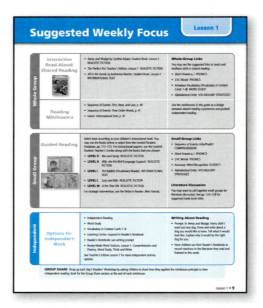

◀ Select from the options for independent work that align with instructional goals.

INDEPENDENT READING The best way to develop reading skills is to read more. Independent reading is a time for children to explore their interests, select books that are "just right" for them, and read continuous text for an established period of time. Support your students as they make book choices because too-hard books will only frustrate them. Teach them how to choose books that they can read with understanding and that don't present too many challenges. Having a large, accessible collection of books—whether in your classroom or in the library—is the best way to support readers.

6 • Independent Literacy Work

Journeys RESOURCES TO SUPPORT INDEPENDENT LITERACY WORK
- Student Book Audiotext CD
- Vocabulary in Context Cards
- Ready-Made Work Stations

READER'S NOTEBOOK A Reader's Notebook is a place for children to respond to their reading and to provide evidence of their understanding. The options for what children may write are endless—letters to you, lists, stories, poems, and journal entries. You may ask them to write about something specific or leave it open for the child to choose. A suggested prompt that links to the week's reading is provided on each Suggested Weekly Focus page.

LISTENING CENTER Using a Listening Center will improve children's listening comprehension and expand their vocabulary. It is also an effective way to have children listen to models of fluent reading. Children may respond to the story or book in their Reader's Notebook.

LETTER/WORD STUDY Expose children to a wide variety of meaningful word study activities. Letter sorting, word sorting, compound words, synonyms and antonyms, and using context clues are just some examples of topics that can be developed into independent literacy activities. The Vocabulary in Context Cards for a given lesson contain words used in the week's literature. On the back of each card, a student-friendly explanation of the word and activities are provided to help children think about how the word can be used in various contexts.

▲ Vocabulary in Context Cards

READY-MADE WORK STATIONS The *Journeys* Ready-Made Work Stations link to the week's literature and skills in three strands of literacy instruction: comprehension and fluency, word study, and writing. Three different activities are provided on each card, providing children with multiple opportunities to practice the skill.

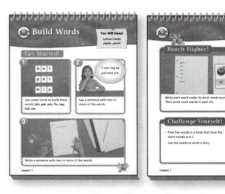

▲ Ready-Made Work Stations

Independent Literacy Work • 7

Planning for Comprehensive Language and Literacy Instruction

Effective teaching begins with careful observation of your students' literacy behaviors, systematic initial and ongoing assessment, and thoughtful planning to meet the literacy needs of your students. In this guide, you will find a consistent structure and a rich collection of resources with a menu of items and lessons to guide your teaching. You will need to tailor your teaching decisions within the lessons to fit the strengths and needs of your particular students.

On the pages that follow, you will find a Suggested Weekly Focus for each lesson. Options are included for each part of the Readers' Workshop.

- **Whole-Group Teaching:** Interactive Read-Aloud/Shared Reading, Reading Minilessons, Suggested Links for Teaching and Reinforcing Skills
- **Small-Group Teaching:** Guided Reading and Literature Discussion, Suggested Links for Teaching and Reinforcing Skills
- **Independent Work:** Independent Reading, Writing About Reading, Word Study, Ready-Made Work Stations, Vocabulary in Context Cards

Suggested Weekly Focus

Lesson 1	9	Lesson 16	24
Lesson 2	10	Lesson 17	25
Lesson 3	11	Lesson 18	26
Lesson 4	12	Lesson 19	27
Lesson 5	13	Lesson 20	28
Lesson 6	14	Lesson 21	29
Lesson 7	15	Lesson 22	30
Lesson 8	16	Lesson 23	31
Lesson 9	17	Lesson 24	32
Lesson 10	18	Lesson 25	33
Lesson 11	19	Lesson 26	34
Lesson 12	20	Lesson 27	35
Lesson 13	21	Lesson 28	36
Lesson 14	22	Lesson 29	37
Lesson 15	23	Lesson 30	38

Suggested Weekly Focus

Lesson 1

Whole Group

Interactive Read-Aloud/Shared Reading

- *Henry and Mudge* by Cynthia Rylant, Student Book: Lesson 1 REALISTIC FICTION
- *The Perfect Pet*, Teacher's Edition: Lesson 1 REALISTIC FICTION
- *All in the Family* by Katherine Mackin, Student Book: Lesson 1 INFORMATIONAL TEXT

Whole-Group Links

You may use the suggested links to teach and reinforce skills in shared reading.

- *Short Vowels* a, i PHONICS
- *CVC Words* PHONICS
- *Introduce Vocabulary (Vocabulary in Context Cards 1–8)* WORD STUDY
- *Alphabetical Order* VOCABULARY STRATEGIES

Reading Minilessons

- Sequence of Events: First, Next, and Last, p. 40
- Sequence of Events: Time-Order Words, p. 41
- Genre: Informational Text, p. 41

Use the minilessons in this guide as a bridge between shared reading experiences and guided/independent reading.

Small Group

Guided Reading

Select texts according to your children's instructional level. You may use the books below or select from the Leveled Readers Database, pp. 112–123. For instructional support, use the Leveled Readers Teacher's Guides along with the books that you choose.

- **LEVEL H** *Ben and Sooty* REALISTIC FICTION
- **LEVEL H** *Billy, the Pet Bird* (Language Support) REALISTIC FICTION
- **LEVEL I** *Pet Rabbits* (Vocabulary Reader) INFORMATIONAL TEXT
- **LEVEL L** *Lucy and Billy* REALISTIC FICTION
- **LEVEL M** *A Pet That Fits* REALISTIC FICTION

For strategic intervention, use the Write-In Reader: *Best Friends*.

Small-Group Links

- *Sequence of Events; Infer/Predict* COMPREHENSION
- *Short Vowels* a, i PHONICS
- *CVC Words* PHONICS
- *Accuracy: Word Recognition* FLUENCY
- *Alphabetical Order* VOCABULARY STRATEGIES

Literature Discussion

You may want to call together small groups for literature discussion. See pp. 124–128 for suggested trade book titles.

Independent

Options for Independent Work

- Independent Reading
- Word Study
- Vocabulary in Context Cards 1–8
- Listening Center: respond in Reader's Notebook
- Reader's Notebook: see writing prompt
- Ready-Made Work Stations, Lesson 1: Comprehension and Fluency, Word Study, Think and Write

See Teacher's Edition Lesson 1 for more independent activity options.

Writing About Reading

- Prompt: In *Henry and Mudge*, Henry didn't want just any dog. Draw and write about a dog you would like to have. Tell what it would look like. Explain why it would be the right dog for you.
- Have children use their Reader's Notebook to record reactions to the literature they read and listened to this week.

GROUP SHARE Wrap up each day's Readers' Workshop by asking children to share how they applied the minilesson principle to their independent reading. Look for the Group Share section at the end of each minilesson.

Suggested Weekly Focus

Lesson 2

Whole Group

Interactive Read-Aloud/Shared Reading

- *My Family* by George Ancona, Student Book: Lesson 2 INFORMATIONAL TEXT
- *More Than a Best Friend*, Teacher's Edition: Lesson 2 INFORMATIONAL TEXT
- *Family Poetry*, Student Book: Lesson 2 POETRY

Whole-Group Links

You may use the suggested links to teach and reinforce skills in shared reading.

- *Short Vowels* o, u, e PHONICS
- *Review CVC Words* PHONICS
- *Introduce Vocabulary (Vocabulary in Context Cards 9–16)* WORD STUDY
- *Using a Glossary* VOCABULARY STRATEGIES

Reading Minilessons

- Compare and Contrast: Same and Different, p. 42
- Compare and Contrast: Same and Different, p. 43
- Genre: Poetry, p. 43

Use the minilessons in this guide as a bridge between shared reading experiences and guided/independent reading.

Small Group

Guided Reading

Select texts according to your children's instructional level. You may use the books below or select from the Leveled Readers Database, pp. 112–123. For instructional support, use the Leveled Readers Teacher's Guides along with the books that you choose.

- **LEVEL F** *Who Is in Your Family?* (Vocabulary Reader) INFORMATIONAL TEXT
- **LEVEL I** *Let's Make Music!* INFORMATIONAL TEXT
- **LEVEL J** *Birthdays Around the World* (Language Support) INFORMATIONAL TEXT
- **LEVEL J** *Happy Birthday, Everyone* INFORMATIONAL TEXT
- **LEVEL N** *How to Make a Family Tree* INFORMATIONAL TEXT

For strategic intervention, use the Write-In Reader: *The Nicest Party*.

Small-Group Links

- *Compare and Contrast; Question* COMPREHENSION
- *Short Vowels* o, u, e PHONICS
- *Review CVC Words* PHONICS
- *Accuracy: Words Connected in Text* FLUENCY
- *Using a Glossary* VOCABULARY STRATEGIES

Literature Discussion

You may want to call together small groups for literature discussion. See pp. 124–128 for suggested trade book titles.

Independent

Options for Independent Work

- Independent Reading
- Word Study
- Vocabulary in Context Cards 9–16
- Listening Center: respond in Reader's Notebook
- Reader's Notebook: see writing prompt
- Ready-Made Work Stations, Lesson 2: Comprehension and Fluency, Word Study, Think and Write

See Teacher's Edition Lesson 2 for more independent activity options.

Writing About Reading

- Prompt: *My Family* tells about Camila's family. Write a story that tells about your family. Draw pictures to go with your story.
- Have children use their Reader's Notebook to record reactions to the literature they read and listened to this week.

GROUP SHARE Wrap up each day's Readers' Workshop by asking children to share how they applied the minilesson principle to their independent reading. Look for the Group Share section at the end of each minilesson.

Suggested Weekly Focus

Lesson 3

Whole Group

Interactive Read-Aloud/ Shared Reading

- *Henry and Mudge Under the Yellow Moon* by Cynthia Rylant, Student Book: Lesson 3 REALISTIC FICTION
- *The Owl Hunt*, Teacher's Edition: Lesson 3 FANTASY
- *Outdoor Adventures*, Student Book: Lesson 3 INFORMATIONAL TEXT

Whole-Group Links

You may use the suggested links to teach and reinforce skills in shared reading.

- *Long Vowels a, i (VCe)* PHONICS
- *Hard and Soft Sounds for c* PHONICS
- *Introduce Vocabulary (Vocabulary in Context Cards 17–24)* WORD STUDY
- *Multiple-Meaning Words* VOCABULARY STRATEGIES

Reading Minilessons

- Author's Purpose: How Authors Write to Help Readers Enjoy the Story, p. 44
- Genre: Fantasy, p. 45
- Text and Graphic Features: Pictures and Labels, p. 45

Use the minilessons in this guide as a bridge between shared reading experiences and guided/independent reading.

Small Group

Guided Reading

Select texts according to your children's instructional level. You may use the books below or select from the Leveled Readers Database, pp. 112–123. For instructional support, use the Leveled Readers Teacher's Guides along with the books that you choose.

- **LEVEL I** *Chipmunks Do What Chipmunks Do* FANTASY
- **LEVEL I** *The Colors of Leaves* (Language Support) FANTASY
- **LEVEL I** *Fall Harvest* (Vocabulary Reader) INFORMATIONAL TEXT
- **LEVEL K** *How the Leaves Got Their Colors* FANTASY
- **LEVEL L** *Annie's Pictures* REALISTIC FICTION

For strategic intervention, use the Write-In Reader: *Too Little For Camping.*

Small-Group Links

- *Author's Purpose; Analyze/Evaluate* COMPREHENSION
- *Long Vowels a, i (VCe)* PHONICS
- *Hard and Soft Sounds for c* PHONICS
- *Accuracy: Self-Correct* FLUENCY
- *Multiple-Meaning Words* VOCABULARY STRATEGIES

Literature Discussion

You may want to call together small groups for literature discussion. See pp. 124–128 for suggested trade book titles.

Independent

Options for Independent Work

- Independent Reading
- Word Study
- Vocabulary in Context Cards 17–24
- Listening Center: respond in Reader's Notebook
- Reader's Notebook: see writing prompt
- Ready-Made Work Stations, Lesson 3: Comprehension and Fluency, Word Study, Think and Write

See Teacher's Edition Lesson 3 for more independent activity options.

Writing About Reading

- Prompt: In *Outdoor Adventures,* Lola and her *Abuelita* sent each other e-mails about what they were doing outside. Write an e-mail like Lola's to a family member or friend. Tell about something you like to do outside. Include a picture with words that tell about it.
- Have children use their Reader's Notebook to record reactions to the literature they read and listened to this week.

GROUP SHARE Wrap up each day's Readers' Workshop by asking children to share how they applied the minilesson principle to their independent reading. Look for the Group Share section at the end of each minilesson.

Suggested Weekly Focus

Lesson 4

Whole Group

Interactive Read-Aloud/Shared Reading

- *Diary of a Spider* by Doreen Cronin, Student Book: Lesson 4 HUMOROUS FICTION
- *Bats: Beastly or Beautiful?*, Teacher's Edition: Lesson 4 INFORMATIONAL TEXT
- *A Swallow and a Spider* retold by Sheila Higginson, Student Book: Lesson 4 FABLE

Whole-Group Links

You may use the suggested links to teach and reinforce skills in shared reading.

- *Long Vowels* o, u, e (VCe) PHONICS
- *Hard and Soft Sounds for* g PHONICS
- *Introduce Vocabulary (Vocabulary in Context Cards 25–32)* WORD STUDY
- *Context Clues* VOCABULARY STRATEGIES

Reading Minilessons

- Cause and Effect: One Event Makes Another Happen, p. 46
- Cause and Effect: One Event Makes Another Happen, p. 47
- Genre: Fable, p. 47

Use the minilessons in this guide as a bridge between shared reading experiences and guided/independent reading.

Small Group

Guided Reading

Select texts according to your children's instructional level. You may use the books below or select from the Leveled Readers Database, pp. 112–123. For instructional support, use the Leveled Readers Teacher's Guides along with the books that you choose.

- **LEVEL H** *Cub Saves the Day* HUMOROUS FICTION
- **LEVEL J** *Along Came a Spider…* (Vocabulary Reader) INFORMATIONAL TEXT
- **LEVEL J** *Flora the Fly Saves the Spiders* (Language Support) HUMOROUS FICTION
- **LEVEL J** *Fly to the Rescue!* HUMOROUS FICTION
- **LEVEL N** *Ferdinand Saves the Day* HUMOROUS FICTION

For strategic intervention, use the Write-In Reader: *Diva the Dancer.*

Small-Group Links

- *Cause and Effect; Summarize* COMPREHENSION
- *Long Vowels* o, u, e (VCe) PHONICS
- *Hard and Soft Sounds for* g PHONICS
- *Intonation* FLUENCY
- *Context Clues* VOCABULARY STRATEGIES

Literature Discussion

You may want to call together small groups for literature discussion. See pp. 124–128 for suggested trade book titles.

Independent

Options for Independent Work

- Independent Reading
- Word Study
- Vocabulary in Context Cards 25–32
- Listening Center: respond in Reader's Notebook
- Reader's Notebook: see writing prompt
- Ready-Made Work Stations, Lesson 4: Comprehension and Fluency, Word Study, Think and Write

See Teacher's Edition Lesson 4 for more independent activity options.

Writing About Reading

- Prompt: In *Diary of a Spider,* Spider writes about different things that happened in his life. Write to tell about what happened in your life over the past few days.
- Have children use their Reader's Notebook to record reactions to the literature they read and listened to this week.

GROUP SHARE Wrap up each day's Readers' Workshop by asking children to share how they applied the minilesson principle to their independent reading. Look for the Group Share section at the end of each minilesson.

Suggested Weekly Focus

Lesson 5

Whole Group

Interactive Read-Aloud/ Shared Reading

- *Teacher's Pets* by Dayle Ann Dodds, Student Book: Lesson 5 REALISTIC FICTION
- *Lester,* Teacher's Edition: Lesson 5 REALISTIC FICTION
- *See Westburg by Bus!,* Student Book: Lesson 5 INFORMATIONAL TEXT

Whole-Group Links

You may use the suggested links to teach and reinforce skills in shared reading.

- *Consonant Blends with* r, l, s PHONICS
- *Introduce Vocabulary (Vocabulary in Context Cards 33–40)* WORD STUDY
- *Base Words and Endings* -ed, -ing VOCABULARY STRATEGIES

Reading Minilessons

- Story Structure: Important Events, p. 48
- Story Structure: Problem, p. 49
- Genre: Informational Text, p. 49

Use the minilessons in this guide as a bridge between shared reading experiences and guided/independent reading.

Small Group

Guided Reading

Select texts according to your children's instructional level. You may use the books below or select from the Leveled Readers Database, pp. 112–123. For instructional support, use the Leveled Readers Teacher's Guides along with the books that you choose.

- **LEVEL H** *Caty the Caterpillar* REALISTIC FICTION
- **LEVEL H** *Fun Pets* (Vocabulary Reader) INFORMATIONAL TEXT
- **LEVEL J** *Foster's Famous Farm* (Language Support) REALISTIC FICTION
- **LEVEL J** *Foster's Farm* REALISTIC FICTION
- **LEVEL L** *Where is Gus-Gus?* REALISTIC FICTION

For strategic intervention, use the Write-In Reader: *The New Playground.*

Small-Group Links

- *Story Structure; Visualize* COMPREHENSION
- *Consonant Blends with* r, l, s PHONICS
- *Phrasing: Punctuation* FLUENCY
- *Base Words and Endings* -ed, -ing VOCABULARY STRATEGIES

Literature Discussion

You may want to call together small groups for literature discussion. See pp. 124–128 for suggested trade book titles.

Independent

Options for Independent Work

- Independent Reading
- Word Study
- Vocabulary in Context Cards 33–40
- Listening Center: respond in Reader's Notebook
- Reader's Notebook: see writing prompt
- Ready-Made Work Stations, Lesson 5: Comprehension and Fluency, Word Study, Think and Write

See Teacher's Edition Lesson 5 for more independent activity options.

Writing About Reading

- Prompt: In *See Westburg by Bus!,* the author gives steps to follow around the town of Westburg. Write steps to guide a visitor around your school. Write a sentence about each place that tells what you do there.
- Have children use their Reader's Notebook to record reactions to the literature they read and listened to this week.

GROUP SHARE Wrap up each day's Readers' Workshop by asking children to share how they applied the minilesson principle to their independent reading. Look for the Group Share section at the end of each minilesson.

Suggested Weekly Focus

Lesson 6

Whole Group

Interactive Read-Aloud/ Shared Reading

- *Animals Building Homes* by Wendy Perkins, Student Book: Lesson 6 INFORMATIONAL TEXT
- *City Life Is for the Birds*, Teacher's Edition: Lesson 6 INFORMATIONAL TEXT
- *Hiding at the Pond* by Sue LaBella, Student Book: Lesson 6 PLAY

Whole-Group Links

You may use the suggested links to teach and reinforce skills in shared reading.

- *Common Final Blends* nd, ng, nk, nt, ft, xt, mp PHONICS
- *Introduce Vocabulary (Vocabulary in Context Cards 41–48)* WORD STUDY
- *Base Words and Prefixes* un- and re- VOCABULARY STRATEGIES

Reading Minilessons

- Text and Graphic Features: Pictures and Words, p. 50
- Genre: Informational Text, p. 51
- Genre: Play, p. 51

Use the minilessons in this guide as a bridge between shared reading experiences and guided/ independent reading.

Small Group

Guided Reading

Select texts according to your children's instructional level. You may use the books below or select from the Leveled Readers Database, pp. 112–123. For instructional support, use the Leveled Readers Teacher's Guides along with the books that you choose.

- **LEVEL I**   *Amazing Nests* (Vocabulary Reader) INFORMATIONAL TEXT
- **LEVEL I**   *A Busy Beaver* INFORMATIONAL TEXT
- **LEVEL L**   *Bees at Work* (Language Support) INFORMATIONAL TEXT
- **LEVEL L**   *Busy Bees* INFORMATIONAL TEXT
- **LEVEL O**   *The Lives of Ants* INFORMATIONAL TEXT

For strategic intervention, use the Write-In Reader: *Who Made These?*

Small-Group Links

- *Text and Graphic Features; Question* COMPREHENSION
- *Common Final Blends* nd, ng, nk, nt, ft, xt, mp PHONICS
- *Expression* FLUENCY
- *Base Words and Prefixes* un- and re- VOCABULARY STRATEGIES

Literature Discussion

You may want to call together small groups for literature discussion. See pp. 124–128 for suggested trade book titles.

Independent

Options for Independent Work

- Independent Reading
- Word Study
- Vocabulary in Context Cards 41–48
- Listening Center: respond in Reader's Notebook
- Reader's Notebook: see writing prompt
- Ready-Made Work Stations, Lesson 6: Comprehension and Fluency, Word Study, Think and Write

See Teacher's Edition Lesson 6 for more independent activity options.

Writing About Reading

- Prompt: Choose two animals from *Animals Building Homes*. Tell how their homes are the same and how they are different.
- Have children use their Reader's Notebook to record reactions to the literature they read and listened to this week.

GROUP SHARE Wrap up each day's Readers' Workshop by asking children to share how they applied the minilesson principle to their independent reading. Look for the Group Share section at the end of each minilesson.

Suggested Weekly Focus

Lesson 7

Whole Group

Interactive Read-Aloud/Shared Reading

- *The Ugly Vegetables* by Grace Lin, Student Book: Lesson 7 REALISTIC FICTION
- *Trouble in the Lily Garden,* Teacher's Edition: Lesson 7 FANTASY
- *They Really Are GIANT!* by Judy Williams, Student Book: Lesson 7 INFORMATIONAL TEXT

Whole-Group Links

You may use the suggested links to teach and reinforce skills in shared reading.

- *Double Consonants and* ck PHONICS
- *Double Consonants (CVC)* PHONICS
- *Introduce Vocabulary (Vocabulary in Context Cards 49–56)* WORD STUDY
- *Homophones* VOCABULARY STRATEGIES

Reading Minilessons

- Understanding Characters: What Characters Say and Do, p. 52
- Conclusions: What Is Happening in the Story, p. 53
- Genre: Informational Text, p. 53

Use the minilessons in this guide as a bridge between shared reading experiences and guided/independent reading.

Small Group

Guided Reading

Select texts according to your children's instructional level. You may use the books below or select from the Leveled Readers Database, pp. 112–123. For instructional support, use the Leveled Readers Teacher's Guides along with the books that you choose.

- **LEVEL G** *Grandma's Surprise* REALISTIC FICTION
- **LEVEL J** *The Community Garden* REALISTIC FICTION
- **LEVEL J** *Luz and the Garden* (Language Support) REALISTIC FICTION
- **LEVEL J** *The Three Sisters* (Vocabulary Reader) INFORMATIONAL TEXT
- **LEVEL O** *Cross-Country Cousins* REALISTIC FICTION

For strategic intervention, use the Write-In Reader: *Rosa's Garden.*

Small-Group Links

- *Conclusions; Analyze/Evaluate* COMPREHENSION
- *Double Consonants and* ck PHONICS
- *Double Consonants (CVC)* PHONICS
- *Accuracy: Connected Text* FLUENCY
- *Homophones* VOCABULARY STRATEGIES

Literature Discussion

You may want to call together small groups for literature discussion. See pp. 124–128 for suggested trade book titles.

Independent

Options for Independent Work

- Independent Reading
- Word Study
- Vocabulary in Context Cards 49–56
- Listening Center: respond in Reader's Notebook
- Reader's Notebook: see writing prompt
- Ready-Made Work Stations, Lesson 7: Comprehension and Fluency, Word Study, Think and Write

See Teacher's Edition Lesson 7 for more independent activity options.

Writing About Reading

- Prompt: In *The Ugly Vegetables,* the characters make a special soup using vegetables they grew. Think of a special food or meal your family makes. Write a recipe for how to make it. Be sure to tell all the things you need and the steps to make it.
- Have children use their Reader's Notebook to record reactions to the literature they read and listened to this week.

GROUP SHARE Wrap up each day's Readers' Workshop by asking children to share how they applied the minilesson principle to their independent reading. Look for the Group Share section at the end of each minilesson.

Lesson 7 • 15

Suggested Weekly Focus

Lesson 8

Whole Group

Interactive Read-Aloud/ Shared Reading

- *Super Storms* by Seymour Simon, Student Book: Lesson 8 INFORMATIONAL TEXT
- *Floods: Dangerous Water,* Teacher's Edition: Lesson 8 INFORMATIONAL TEXT
- *Weather Poems,* Student Book: Lesson 8 POETRY

Whole-Group Links

You may use the suggested links to teach and reinforce skills in shared reading.

- *Consonant Digraphs* th, sh, wh, ch, tch, ph PHONICS
- *Base Words with Endings* -s,-ed, -ing PHONICS
- *Introduce Vocabulary* (Vocabulary in Context Cards 57–64) WORD STUDY
- *Compound Words* VOCABULARY STRATEGIES

Reading Minilessons

- Main Idea and Details: What the Text Is Mostly About, p. 54
- Main Idea and Details: What the Text Is Mostly About, p. 55
- Genre: Poetry, p. 55

Use the minilessons in this guide as a bridge between shared reading experiences and guided/ independent reading.

Small Group

Guided Reading

Select texts according to your children's instructional level. You may use the books below or select from the Leveled Readers Database, pp. 112–123. For instructional support, use the Leveled Readers Teacher's Guides along with the books that you choose.

- **LEVEL G**   *A Snowy Day* INFORMATIONAL TEXT
- **LEVEL I**   *Let It Rain!* (Vocabulary Reader) INFORMATIONAL TEXT
- **LEVEL L**   *What Is in the Wind?* INFORMATIONAL TEXT
- **LEVEL L**   *The Wind* (Language Support) INFORMATIONAL TEXT
- **LEVEL N**   *Lessons About Lightning* INFORMATIONAL TEXT

For strategic intervention, use the Write-In Reader: *Keeping Safe in a Storm.*

Small-Group Links

- *Main Idea and Details; Visualize* COMPREHENSION
- *Consonant Digraphs* th, sh, wh, ch, tch, ph PHONICS
- *Base Words with Endings* -s,-ed, -ing PHONICS
- *Rate* FLUENCY
- *Compound Words* VOCABULARY STRATEGIES

Literature Discussion

You may want to call together small groups for literature discussion. See pp. 124–128 for suggested trade book titles.

Independent

Options for Independent Work

- Independent Reading
- Word Study
- Vocabulary in Context Cards 57–64
- Listening Center: respond in Reader's Notebook
- Reader's Notebook: see writing prompt
- Ready-Made Work Stations, Lesson 8: Comprehension and Fluency, Word Study, Think and Write

See Teacher's Edition Lesson 8 for more independent activity options.

Writing About Reading

- Prompt: This week you read some poems about weather. Write your own poem about weather. Use words that tell what the weather looks, feels, sounds, tastes, and smells like.
- Have children use their Reader's Notebook to record reactions to the literature they read and listened to this week.

GROUP SHARE Wrap up each day's Readers' Workshop by asking children to share how they applied the minilesson principle to their independent reading. Look for the Group Share section at the end of each minilesson.

16 • Lesson 8

Suggested Weekly Focus

Lesson 9

Whole Group

Interactive Read-Aloud/Shared Reading

- *How Chipmunk Got His Stripes* by Joseph Bruchac and James Bruchac, Student Book: Lesson 9 FOLKTALE
- *On Thin Ice,* Teacher's Edition: Lesson 9 FOLKTALE
- *Why Rabbits Have Short Tails* adapted by Gina Sabella, Student Book: Lesson 9 FOLKTALE

Whole-Group Links

You may use the suggested links to teach and reinforce skills in shared reading.

- *Base Words and Endings* -ed, -ing PHONICS
- *CV Words* PHONICS
- *Introduce Vocabulary (Vocabulary in Context Cards 65–72)* WORD STUDY
- *Synonyms* VOCABULARY STRATEGIES

Reading Minilessons

- Understanding Characters: What Characters Say and Do, p. 56
- Understanding Characters: What Characters Do and Why, p. 57
- Genre: Folktale, p. 57

Use the minilessons in this guide as a bridge between shared reading experiences and guided/independent reading.

Small Group

Guided Reading

Select texts according to your children's instructional level. You may use the books below or select from the Leveled Readers Database, pp. 112–123. For instructional support, use the Leveled Readers Teacher's Guides along with the books that you choose.

- **LEVEL I**   *Camel's Hump* FOLKTALE
- **LEVEL J**   *Native American Folktales* (Vocabulary Reader) INFORMATIONAL TEXT
- **LEVEL K**   *How Coyote Stole Fire* FOLKTALE
- **LEVEL K**   *How People Got Fire* (Language Support) FOLKTALE
- **LEVEL N**   *Uncle Rabbit* FOLKTALE

For strategic intervention, use the Write-In Reader: *Tortoise Gets a Home.*

Small-Group Links

- *Understanding Characters; Summarize* COMPREHENSION
- *Base Words and Endings* -ed, -ing PHONICS
- *CV Words* PHONICS
- *Phrasing: Punctuation* FLUENCY
- *Synonyms* VOCABULARY STRATEGIES

Literature Discussion

You may want to call together small groups for literature discussion. See pp. 124–128 for suggested trade book titles.

Independent

Options for Independent Work

- Independent Reading
- Word Study
- Vocabulary in Context Cards 65–72
- Listening Center: respond in Reader's Notebook
- Reader's Notebook: see writing prompt
- Ready-Made Work Stations, Lesson 9: Comprehension and Fluency, Word Study, Think and Write

See Teacher's Edition Lesson 9 for more independent activity options.

Writing About Reading

- Prompt: *How Chipmunk Got His Stripes* tells an author's idea about how something in nature came to be. What other things in nature could be explained in a folktale? Write about one of them.
- Have children use their Reader's Notebook to record reactions to the literature they read and listened to this week.

GROUP SHARE Wrap up each day's Readers' Workshop by asking children to share how they applied the minilesson principle to their independent reading. Look for the Group Share section at the end of each minilesson.

Suggested Weekly Focus

Lesson 10

Whole Group

Interactive Read-Aloud/Shared Reading

- *Jellies* by Twig C. George, Student Book: Lesson 10 INFORMATIONAL TEXT
- *Sharks on the Run!*, Teacher's Edition: Lesson 10 INFORMATIONAL TEXT
- *Meet Norbert Wu*, Student Book: Lesson 10 INFORMATIONAL TEXT

Whole-Group Links

You may use the suggested links to teach and reinforce skills in shared reading.

- *Contractions* PHONICS
- *Introduce Vocabulary (Vocabulary in Context Cards 73–80)* WORD STUDY
- *Base Words and Suffixes* -er, -est VOCABULARY STRATEGIES

Reading Minilessons

- Fact and Opinion: What Can Be Proved Versus What the Author Thinks, p. 58
- Fact and Opinion: Words That Show How an Author Feels, p. 59
- Text and Graphic Features: Pictures and Words, p. 59

Use the minilessons in this guide as a bridge between shared reading experiences and guided/independent reading.

Small Group

Guided Reading

Select texts according to your children's instructional level. You may use the books below or select from the Leveled Readers Database, pp. 112–123. For instructional support, use the Leveled Readers Teacher's Guides along with the books that you choose.

- **LEVEL H** *Animals at the Aquarium* INFORMATIONAL TEXT
- **LEVEL I** *Coral Reefs* (Vocabulary Reader) INFORMATIONAL TEXT
- **LEVEL K** *Life in Tide Pools* INFORMATIONAL TEXT
- **LEVEL K** *Tide Pools* (Language Support) INFORMATIONAL TEXT
- **LEVEL O** *Bottlenose Dolphins* INFORMATIONAL TEXT

For strategic intervention, use the Write-In Reader: *At the Beach*.

Small-Group Links

- *Fact and Opinion; Monitor/Clarify* COMPREHENSION
- *Contractions* PHONICS
- *Stress* FLUENCY
- *Base Words and Suffixes* -er, -est VOCABULARY STRATEGIES

Literature Discussion

You may want to call together small groups for literature discussion. See pp. 124–128 for suggested trade book titles.

Independent

Options for Independent Work

- Independent Reading
- Word Study
- Vocabulary in Context Cards 73–80
- Listening Center: respond in Reader's Notebook
- Reader's Notebook: see writing prompt
- Ready-Made Work Stations, Lesson 10: Comprehension and Fluency, Word Study, Think and Write

See Teacher's Edition Lesson 10 for more independent activity options.

Writing About Reading

- Prompt: In *Jellies,* the author uses words and pictures to show what different jellyfish are like. Choose one jellyfish, and write a poem about it. Use words that tell how the jellyfish looks and moves.
- Have children use their Reader's Notebook to record reactions to the literature they read and listened to this week.

GROUP SHARE Wrap up each day's Readers' Workshop by asking children to share how they applied the minilesson principle to their independent reading. Look for the Group Share section at the end of each minilesson.

Suggested Weekly Focus

Lesson 11

Whole Group

Interactive Read-Aloud/ Shared Reading

- *Click, Clack, Moo: Cows That Type* by Doreen Cronin, Student Book: Lesson 11 HUMOROUS FICTION
- *Don't Play Cards with a Dog in the Room!*, Teacher's Edition: Lesson 11 INFORMATIONAL TEXT
- *Talk About Smart Animals!* by Donald Logan, Student Book: Lesson 11 INFORMATIONAL TEXT

Whole-Group Links

You may use the suggested links to teach and reinforce skills in shared reading.

- *Base Words with Endings* -s, -es PHONICS
- *Introduce Vocabulary (Vocabulary in Context Cards 81–88)* WORD STUDY
- *Prefixes* pre- *and* mis- VOCABULARY STRATEGIES

Reading Minilessons

- Conclusions: Clues That Show How Characters Feel, p. 60
- Conclusions: How an Author Feels About the Topic, p. 61
- Text and Graphic Features: Headings, p. 61

Use the minilessons in this guide as a bridge between shared reading experiences and guided/independent reading.

Small Group

Guided Reading

Select texts according to your children's instructional level. You may use the books below or select from the Leveled Readers Database, pp. 112–123. For instructional support, use the Leveled Readers Teacher's Guides along with the books that you choose.

- **LEVEL H** *Zoo Party* HUMOROUS FICTION
- **LEVEL J** *The Smiths and Their Animals* (Language Support) HUMOROUS FICTION
- **LEVEL K** *From Typewriters to Computers* (Vocabulary Reader) INFORMATIONAL TEXT
- **LEVEL K** *Pay Attention!* HUMOROUS FICTION
- **LEVEL N** *E-Mails from the Teacher* HUMOROUS FICTION

For strategic intervention, use the Write-In Reader: *The Play Date*.

Small-Group Links

- *Conclusions; Infer/Predict* COMPREHENSION
- *Base Words with Endings* -s, -es PHONICS
- *Expression* FLUENCY
- *Prefixes* pre- *and* mis- VOCABULARY STRATEGIES

Literature Discussion

You may want to call together small groups for literature discussion. See pp. 124–128 for suggested trade book titles.

Independent

Options for Independent Work

- Independent Reading
- Word Study
- Vocabulary in Context Cards 81–88
- Listening Center: respond in Reader's Notebook
- Reader's Notebook: see writing prompt
- Ready-Made Work Stations, Lesson 11: Comprehension and Fluency, Word Study, Think and Write

See Teacher's Edition Lesson 11 for more independent activity options.

Writing About Reading

- Prompt: Imagine you are an animal on a farm. Write a letter to the farmer asking for something that would make your life more fun.
- Have children use their Reader's Notebook to record reactions to the literature they read and listened to this week.

GROUP SHARE Wrap up each day's Readers' Workshop by asking children to share how they applied the minilesson principle to their independent reading. Look for the Group Share section at the end of each minilesson.

Suggested Weekly Focus

Lesson 12

Whole Group

Interactive Read-Aloud/ Shared Reading

- *Violet's Music* by Angela Johnson, Student Book: Lesson 12 REALISTIC FICTION
- *Rita Breaks the Rules,* Teacher's Edition: Lesson 12 REALISTIC FICTION
- *Wolfgang Mozart, Child Superstar* by Mark Bechelli, Student Book: Lesson 12 BIOGRAPHY

Whole-Group Links

You may use the suggested links to teach and reinforce skills in shared reading.

- *Vowel Digraphs* ai, ay PHONICS
- *Introduce Vocabulary (Vocabulary in Context Cards 89–96)* WORD STUDY
- *Figurative Language/Idioms* VOCABULARY STRATEGIES

Reading Minilessons

- Story Structure: Problem, p. 62
- Story Structure: Setting, p. 63
- Genre: Biography, p. 63

Use the minilessons in this guide as a bridge between shared reading experiences and guided/ independent reading.

Small Group

Guided Reading

Select texts according to your children's instructional level. You may use the books below or select from the Leveled Readers Database, pp. 112–123. For instructional support, use the Leveled Readers Teacher's Guides along with the books that you choose.

- **LEVEL G** *A Real Band* REALISTIC FICTION
- **LEVEL I** *Bongos, Maracas, and Xylophones* (Vocabulary Reader) INFORMATIONAL TEXT
- **LEVEL J** *Rosa the Painter* (Language Support) REALISTIC FICTION
- **LEVEL J** *What Can Rosa Paint?* REALISTIC FICTION
- **LEVEL O** *A Thousand Words* REALISTIC FICTION

For strategic intervention, use the Write-In Reader: *Val's Voice.*

Small-Group Links

- *Story Structure; Question* COMPREHENSION
- *Vowel Digraphs* ai, ay PHONICS
- *Intonation* FLUENCY
- *Figurative Language/Idioms* VOCABULARY STRATEGIES

Literature Discussion

You may want to call together small groups for literature discussion. See pp. 124–128 for suggested trade book titles.

Independent

Options for Independent Work

- Independent Reading
- Word Study
- Vocabulary in Context Cards 89–96
- Listening Center: respond in Reader's Notebook
- Reader's Notebook: see writing prompt
- Ready-Made Work Stations, Lesson 12: Comprehension and Fluency, Word Study, Think and Write

See Teacher's Edition Lesson 12 for more independent activity options.

Writing About Reading

- Prompt: Imagine that Violet from *Violet's Music* met young Wolfgang Mozart. Write about what they would say to each other.
- Have children use their Reader's Notebook to record reactions to the literature they read and listened to this week.

GROUP SHARE Wrap up each day's Readers' Workshop by asking children to share how they applied the minilesson principle to their independent reading. Look for the Group Share section at the end of each minilesson.

Suggested Weekly Focus

Lesson 13

Whole Group

Interactive Read-Aloud/Shared Reading

- *Schools Around the World* by Margaret C. Hall, Student Book: Lesson 13 INFORMATIONAL TEXT
- *One-Room Schoolhouse*, Teacher's Edition: Lesson 13 INFORMATIONAL TEXT
- *School Poems*, Student Book: Lesson 13 POETRY

Whole-Group Links

You may use the suggested links to teach and reinforce skills in shared reading.

- *Vowel Digraphs* ee, ea PHONICS
- *Introduce Vocabulary (Vocabulary in Context Cards 97–104)* WORD STUDY
- *Using a Dictionary* VOCABULARY STRATEGIES

Reading Minilessons

- Author's Purpose: Why the Author Wrote the Book, p. 64
- Genre: Informational Text, p. 65
- Genre: Poetry, p. 65

Use the minilessons in this guide as a bridge between shared reading experiences and guided/independent reading.

Small Group

Guided Reading

Select texts according to your children's instructional level. You may use the books below or select from the Leveled Readers Database, pp. 112–123. For instructional support, use the Leveled Readers Teacher's Guides along with the books that you choose.

- **LEVEL I** *One Room Schools* (Vocabulary Reader) INFORMATIONAL TEXT
- **LEVEL J** *Guide Dog School* INFORMATIONAL TEXT
- **LEVEL K** *What School Was Like Long Ago* (Language Support) INFORMATIONAL TEXT
- **LEVEL M** *School Long Ago* INFORMATIONAL TEXT
- **LEVEL N** *A School in a Garden* INFORMATIONAL TEXT

For strategic intervention, use the Write-In Reader: *Game Time!*

Small-Group Links

- *Author's Purpose; Analyze/Evaluate* COMPREHENSION
- *Vowel Digraphs* ee, ea PHONICS
- *Stress* FLUENCY
- *Using a Dictionary* VOCABULARY STRATEGIES

Literature Discussion

You may want to call together small groups for literature discussion. See pp. 124-128 for suggested trade book titles.

Independent

Options for Independent Work

- Independent Reading
- Word Study
- Vocabulary in Context Cards 97–104
- Listening Center: respond in Reader's Notebook
- Reader's Notebook: see writing prompt
- Ready-Made Work Stations, Lesson 13: Comprehension and Fluency, Word Study, Think and Write

See Teacher's Edition Lesson 13 for more independent activity options.

Writing About Reading

- Prompt: This week you read some poems about school. Write your own poem about what school is like for you. Use words that tell how things look, feel, taste, sound, and smell.
- Have children use their Reader's Notebook to record reactions to the literature they read and listened to this week.

GROUP SHARE Wrap up each day's Readers' Workshop by asking children to share how they applied the minilesson principle to their independent reading. Look for the Group Share section at the end of each minilesson.

Suggested Weekly Focus

Lesson 14

Whole Group

Interactive Read-Aloud/Shared Reading

- *Helen Keller* by Jane Sutcliffe, Student Book: Lesson 14 BIOGRAPHY
- *Whale of a Lesson*, Teacher's Edition: Lesson 14 INFORMATIONAL TEXT
- *Talking Tools*, Student Book: Lesson 14 INFORMATIONAL TEXT

Whole-Group Links

You may use the suggested links to teach and reinforce skills in shared reading.

- *Long* o (o, oa, ow) PHONICS
- Introduce Vocabulary (Vocabulary in Context Cards 105–112) WORD STUDY
- *Suffix* -ly VOCABULARY STRATEGIES

Reading Minilessons

- Main Idea and Details: The Most Important Things That Happened in a Person's Life, p. 66
- Main Idea and Details: How the Author Tells About One Idea, p. 67
- Text and Graphic Features: Words and Pictures, p. 67

Use the minilessons in this guide as a bridge between shared reading experiences and guided/independent reading.

Small Group

Guided Reading

Select texts according to your children's instructional level. You may use the books below or select from the Leveled Readers Database, pp. 112–123. For instructional support, use the Leveled Readers Teacher's Guides along with the books that you choose.

- **LEVEL J**   *Anne Sullivan* BIOGRAPHY
- **LEVEL J**   *Special Tools* (Vocabulary Reader) INFORMATIONAL TEXT
- **LEVEL M**   *Alexander Graham Bell* BIOGRAPHY
- **LEVEL M**   *Inventor of the Telephone* (Language Support) BIOGRAPHY
- **LEVEL O**   *The Adventures of Erik* BIOGRAPHY

For strategic intervention, use the Write-In Reader: *Louis Braille*.

Small-Group Links

- Main Idea and Details; Summarize COMPREHENSION
- *Long* o (o, oa, ow) PHONICS
- Natural Pauses FLUENCY
- *Suffix* -ly VOCABULARY STRATEGIES

Literature Discussion

You may want to call together small groups for literature discussion. See pp. 124–128 for suggested trade book titles.

Independent

Options for Independent Work

- Independent Reading
- Word Study
- Vocabulary in Context Cards 105–112
- Listening Center: respond in Reader's Notebook
- Reader's Notebook: see writing prompt
- Ready-Made Work Stations, Lesson 14: Comprehension and Fluency, Word Study, Think and Write

See Teacher's Edition Lesson 14 for more independent activity options.

Writing About Reading

- Prompt: Imagine you could meet Helen Keller. Write a list of questions that you would ask her about her life.
- Have children use their Reader's Notebook to record reactions to the literature they read and listened to this week.

GROUP SHARE Wrap up each day's Readers' Workshop by asking children to share how they applied the minilesson principle to their independent reading. Look for the Group Share section at the end of each minilesson.

Suggested Weekly Focus

Lesson 15

Whole Group

Interactive Read-Aloud/ Shared Reading

- *Officer Buckle and Gloria* by Peggy Rathmann, Student Book: Lesson 15 HUMOROUS FICTION
- *Adventures at Scout Camp,* Teacher's Edition: Lesson 15 REALISTIC FICTION
- *Safety at Home* by Margaret Sweeny, Student Book: Lesson 15 READERS' THEATER/PLAY

Whole-Group Links

You may use the suggested links to teach and reinforce skills in shared reading.

- *Compound Words* PHONICS
- *Schwa Vowel Sound* PHONICS
- *Introduce Vocabulary (Vocabulary in Context Cards 113–120)* WORD STUDY
- *Dictionary Entry* VOCABULARY STRATEGIES

Reading Minilessons

- Cause and Effect: One Thing Makes Another Happen, p. 68
- Cause and Effect: One Thing Makes Another Happen, p. 69
- Genre: Play, p. 69

Use the minilessons in this guide as a bridge between shared reading experiences and guided/independent reading.

Small Group

Guided Reading

Select texts according to your children's instructional level. You may use the books below or select from the Leveled Readers Database, pp. 112–123. For instructional support, use the Leveled Readers Teacher's Guides along with the books that you choose.

- **LEVEL G** *Firedog!* HUMOROUS FICTION
- **LEVEL I** *Police in the Community* (Vocabulary Reader) INFORMATIONAL TEXT
- **LEVEL J** *The Best Student* (Language Support) HUMOROUS FICTION
- **LEVEL J** *Good Citizen* HUMOROUS FICTION
- **LEVEL M** *A Well-Trained Dog* HUMOROUS FICTION

For strategic intervention, use the Write-In Reader: *Fire Safety Day.*

Small-Group Links

- *Cause and Effect; Monitor/Clarify* COMPREHENSION
- *Compound Words* PHONICS
- *Schwa Vowel Sound* PHONICS
- *Accuracy: Connected Text* FLUENCY
- *Dictionary Entry* VOCABULARY STRATEGIES

Literature Discussion

You may want to call together small groups for literature discussion. See pp. 124–128 for suggested trade book titles.

Independent

Options for Independent Work

- Independent Reading
- Word Study
- Vocabulary in Context Cards 113–120
- Listening Center: respond in Reader's Notebook
- Reader's Notebook: see writing prompt
- Ready-Made Work Stations, Lesson 15: Comprehension and Fluency, Word Study, Think and Write

See Teacher's Edition Lesson 15 for more independent activity options.

Writing About Reading

- Prompt: In *Officer Buckle and Gloria,* Officer Buckle writes safety tips and posts them on his bulletin board. Think about what you have learned about staying safe. Choose an activity such as camping, swimming, or biking. Write a list of safety tips for the activity.
- Have children use their Reader's Notebook to record reactions to the literature they read and listened to this week.

GROUP SHARE Wrap up each day's Readers' Workshop by asking children to share how they applied the minilesson principle to their independent reading. Look for the Group Share section at the end of each minilesson.

Suggested Weekly Focus

Lesson 16

Whole Group

Interactive Read-Aloud/ Shared Reading

- *Mr. Tanen's Tie Trouble* by Maryann Cocca-Leffler, Student Book: Lesson 16 REALISTIC FICTION
- *A Better Way to Save,* Teacher's Edition: Lesson 16 REALISTIC FICTION
- *Playground Fun!,* Student Book: Lesson 16 INFORMATIONAL TEXT

Whole-Group Links

You may use the suggested links to teach and reinforce skills in shared reading.

- *Base Words and Endings* -ed, -ing PHONICS
- *Introduce Vocabulary (Vocabulary in Context Cards 121–128)* WORD STUDY
- *Homographs* VOCABULARY STRATEGIES

Reading Minilessons

- Story Structure: Problem and Solution, p. 70
- Story Structure: How the Problem Is Solved, p. 71
- Text and Graphic Features: The Colors and Sizes of Letters, p. 71

Use the minilessons in this guide as a bridge between shared reading experiences and guided/ independent reading.

Small Group

Guided Reading

Select texts according to your children's instructional level. You may use the books below or select from the Leveled Readers Database, pp. 112–123. For instructional support, use the Leveled Readers Teacher's Guides along with the books that you choose.

- **LEVEL I** *Our Library* REALISTIC FICTION
- **LEVEL J** *Raising Funds* (Vocabulary Reader) INFORMATIONAL TEXT
- **LEVEL K** *The Bake Sale* REALISTIC FICTION
- **LEVEL K** *Ms. Hawkins and the Bake Sale* (Language Support) REALISTIC FICTION
- **LEVEL M** *The Town Auction* REALISTIC FICTION

For strategic intervention, use the Write-In Reader: *Kate's Helping Day.*

Small-Group Links

- *Story Structure; Infer/Predict* COMPREHENSION
- *Base Words and Endings* -ed, -ing PHONICS
- *Rate* FLUENCY
- *Homographs* VOCABULARY STRATEGIES

Literature Discussion

You may want to call together small groups for literature discussion. See pp. 124–128 for suggested trade book titles.

Independent

Options for Independent Work

- Independent Reading
- Word Study
- Vocabulary in Context Cards 121–128
- Listening Center: respond in Reader's Notebook
- Reader's Notebook: see writing prompt
- Ready-Made Work Stations, Lesson 16: Comprehension and Fluency, Word Study, Think and Write

See Teacher's Edition Lesson 16 for more independent activity options.

Writing About Reading

- Prompt: In *Mr. Tanen's Tie Trouble*, many things happen to Mr. Tanen. Draw a four-picture comic strip to retell the most important parts of the story. Write sentences under each picture to tell what is happening.
- Have children use their Reader's Notebook to record reactions to the literature they read and listened to this week.

GROUP SHARE Wrap up each day's Readers' Workshop by asking children to share how they applied the minilesson principle to their independent reading. Look for the Group Share section at the end of each minilesson.

Suggested Weekly Focus

Lesson 17

Whole Group

Interactive Read-Aloud/Shared Reading

- *Luke Goes to Bat* by Rachel Isadora, Student Book: Lesson 17 REALISTIC FICTION
- *Tiger Woods: Superstar in Golf and Life,* Teacher's Edition: Lesson 17 BIOGRAPHY
- *Jackie Robinson,* Student Book: Lesson 17 INFORMATIONAL TEXT

Whole-Group Links

You may use the suggested links to teach and reinforce skills in shared reading.

- *Long* i (i, igh, ie, y) PHONICS
- *Introduce Vocabulary (Vocabulary in Context Cards 129–136)* WORD STUDY
- *Antonyms* VOCABULARY STRATEGIES

Reading Minilessons

- Genre: Realistic Fiction, p. 72
- Sequence of Events: What a Person Did, p. 73
- Sequence of Events: Dates and Clue Words, p. 73

Use the minilessons in this guide as a bridge between shared reading experiences and guided/independent reading.

Small Group

Guided Reading

Select texts according to your children's instructional level. You may use the books below or select from the Leveled Readers Database, pp. 112–123. For instructional support, use the Leveled Readers Teacher's Guides along with the books that you choose.

- **LEVEL G** *The Winning Hit* REALISTIC FICTION
- **LEVEL J** *The Brooklyn Dodgers* (Vocabulary Reader) INFORMATIONAL TEXT
- **LEVEL K** *The Summer of Baseball Parks* (Language Support) REALISTIC FICTION
- **LEVEL K** *Take Me Out to the Ballpark* REALISTIC FICTION
- **LEVEL M** *The New Field* REALISTIC FICTION

For strategic intervention, use the Write-In Reader: *True Heroes.*

Small-Group Links

- *Sequence of Events; Visualize* COMPREHENSION
- *Long* i (i, igh, ie, y) PHONICS
- *Stress* FLUENCY
- *Antonyms* VOCABULARY STRATEGIES

Literature Discussion

You may want to call together small groups for literature discussion. See pp. 124–128 for suggested trade book titles.

Independent

Options for Independent Work

- Independent Reading
- Word Study
- Vocabulary in Context Cards 129–136
- Listening Center: respond in Reader's Notebook
- Reader's Notebook: see writing prompt
- Ready-Made Work Stations, Lesson 17: Comprehension and Fluency, Word Study, Think and Write

See Teacher's Edition Lesson 17 for more independent activity options.

Writing About Reading

- Prompt: The baseball player Jackie Robinson appears in both *Luke Goes to Bat* and *Jackie Robinson*. Write a paragraph that tells how the stories are the same and different.
- Have children use their Reader's Notebook to record reactions to the literature they read and listened to this week.

GROUP SHARE Wrap up each day's Readers' Workshop by asking children to share how they applied the minilesson principle to their independent reading. Look for the Group Share section at the end of each minilesson.

Suggested Weekly Focus

Lesson 18

Whole Group

Interactive Read-Aloud/Shared Reading

- *My Name Is Gabriela* by Monica Brown, Student Book: Lesson 18 BIOGRAPHY
- *Doctor Salk's Treasure*, Teacher's Edition: Lesson 18 INFORMATIONAL TEXT
- *Poems About Reading and Writing*, Student Book: Lesson 18 POETRY

Whole-Group Links

You may use the suggested links to teach and reinforce skills in shared reading.

- *Long e Sound for y* PHONICS
- *Changing y to i* PHONICS
- *Introduce Vocabulary (Vocabulary in Context Cards 137–144)* WORD STUDY
- *Suffixes -y and -ful* VOCABULARY STRATEGIES

Reading Minilessons

- Understanding Characters: What Characters Are Like, p. 74
- Cause and Effect: One Thing Makes Other Things Happen, p. 75
- Genre: Poetry, p. 75

Use the minilessons in this guide as a bridge between shared reading experiences and guided/independent reading.

Small Group

Guided Reading

Select texts according to your children's instructional level. You may use the books below or select from the Leveled Readers Database, pp. 112–123. For instructional support, use the Leveled Readers Teacher's Guides along with the books that you choose.

- **LEVEL K** *All About Chile* (Vocabulary Reader) INFORMATIONAL TEXT
- **LEVEL K** *Beatrix Potter* BIOGRAPHY
- **LEVEL M** *Jack Prelutsky* (Language Support) BIOGRAPHY
- **LEVEL M** *The Life of Jack Prelutsky* BIOGRAPHY
- **LEVEL P** *The Life of Langston Hughes* BIOGRAPHY

For strategic intervention, use the Write-In Reader: *Pat Mora*.

Small-Group Links

- *Understanding Characters; Analyze/Evaluate* COMPREHENSION
- *Long e Sound for y* PHONICS
- *Changing y to i* PHONICS
- *Expression* FLUENCY
- *Suffixes -y and -ful* VOCABULARY STRATEGIES

Literature Discussion

You may want to call together small groups for literature discussion. See pp. 124–128 for suggested trade book titles.

Independent

Options for Independent Work

- Independent Reading
- Word Study
- Vocabulary in Context Cards 137–144
- Listening Center: respond in Reader's Notebook
- Reader's Notebook: see writing prompt
- Ready-Made Work Stations, Lesson 18: Comprehension and Fluency, Word Study, Think and Write

See Teacher's Edition Lesson 18 for more independent activity options.

Writing About Reading

- Prompt: Gabriela Mistral liked words such as *fluttering butterfly* that made pictures in her mind. Write three words that you like and then use them in a poem. Be sure that the words help readers make pictures in their minds.
- Have children use their Reader's Notebook to record reactions to the literature they read and listened to this week.

GROUP SHARE Wrap up each day's Readers' Workshop by asking children to share how they applied the minilesson principle to their independent reading. Look for the Group Share section at the end of each minilesson.

Suggested Weekly Focus

Lesson 19

Whole Group

Interactive Read-Aloud/Shared Reading

- *The Signmaker's Assistant* by Tedd Arnold, Student Book: Lesson 19 HUMOROUS FICTION
- *Wild Friends, Wow!*, Teacher's Edition: Lesson 19 INFORMATIONAL TEXT
- *The Trouble with Signs* by Bebe Jaffe, Student Book: Lesson 19 PLAY

Whole-Group Links

You may use the suggested links to teach and reinforce skills in shared reading.

- *r*-Controlled Vowel *ar* PHONICS
- Introduce Vocabulary (Vocabulary in Context Cards 145–152) WORD STUDY
- Synonyms VOCABULARY STRATEGIES

Reading Minilessons

- Text and Graphic Features: Important Information in Art, p. 76
- Genre: Informational Text, p. 77
- Genre: Play, p. 77

Use the minilessons in this guide as a bridge between shared reading experiences and guided/independent reading.

Small Group

Guided Reading

Select texts according to your children's instructional level. You may use the books below or select from the Leveled Readers Database, pp. 112–123. For instructional support, use the Leveled Readers Teacher's Guides along with the books that you choose.

- **LEVEL I** *Aldo and Abby* HUMOROUS FICTION
- **LEVEL J** *Signs Are Everywhere* (Vocabulary Reader) INFORMATIONAL TEXT
- **LEVEL K** *Finding the Party* HUMOROUS FICTION
- **LEVEL K** *Sam Finds the Party* (Language Support) HUMOROUS FICTION
- **LEVEL L** *Too Many Signs!* HUMOROUS FICTION

For strategic intervention, use the Write-In Reader: *The Big City*.

Small-Group Links

- Text and Graphic Features; Question COMPREHENSION
- *r*-Controlled Vowel *ar* PHONICS
- Phrasing: Punctuation FLUENCY
- Synonyms VOCABULARY STRATEGIES

Literature Discussion

You may want to call together small groups for literature discussion. See pp. 124–128 for suggested trade book titles.

Independent

Options for Independent Work

- Independent Reading
- Word Study
- Vocabulary in Context Cards 145–152
- Listening Center: respond in Reader's Notebook
- Reader's Notebook: see writing prompt
- Ready-Made Work Stations, Lesson 19: Comprehension and Fluency, Word Study, Think and Write

See Teacher's Edition Lesson 19 for more independent activity options.

Writing About Reading

- Prompt: In *The Signmaker's Assistant*, Norman puts up silly signs around town. Think of a silly sign you could put up in your school. Write a story about putting up that silly sign. Tell what people do when they read it.
- Have children use their Reader's Notebook to record reactions to the literature they read and listened to this week.

GROUP SHARE Wrap up each day's Readers' Workshop by asking children to share how they applied the minilesson principle to their independent reading. Look for the Group Share section at the end of each minilesson.

Suggested Weekly Focus

Lesson 20

Whole Group

Interactive Read-Aloud/ Shared Reading

- *Dex: The Heart of a Hero* by Caralyn Buehner, Student Book: Lesson 20 FANTASY
- *Ordinary Heroes*, Teacher's Edition: Lesson 20 REALISTIC FICTION
- *Heroes Then and Now*, Student Book: Lesson 20 INFORMATIONAL TEXT

Whole-Group Links

You may use the suggested links to teach and reinforce skills in shared reading.

- r-*Controlled Vowels* or, ore PHONICS
- *Introduce Vocabulary (Vocabulary in Context Cards 153–160)* WORD STUDY
- *Prefix* over- VOCABULARY STRATEGIES

Reading Minilessons

- Compare and Contrast: How Characters Are the Same and Different, p. 78
- Compare and Contrast: How Things Are the Same and Different, p. 79
- Genre: Informational Text, p. 79

Use the minilessons in this guide as a bridge between shared reading experiences and guided/ independent reading.

Small Group

Guided Reading

Select texts according to your children's instructional level. You may use the books below or select from the Leveled Readers Database, pp. 112–123. For instructional support, use the Leveled Readers Teacher's Guides along with the books that you choose.

- **LEVEL I** *Everyday Hero* (Vocabulary Reader) INFORMATIONAL TEXT
- **LEVEL I** *Two Heroes* FANTASY
- **LEVEL J** *Superheroes Save the Day* (Language Support) FANTASY
- **LEVEL J** *Superheroes to the Rescue* FANTASY
- **LEVEL L** *The Mysterious Superhero* FANTASY

For strategic intervention, use the Write-In Reader: *Sue and the Tired Wolf*.

Small-Group Links

- *Compare and Contrast; Monitor/Clarify* COMPREHENSION
- r-*Controlled Vowels* or, ore PHONICS
- *Intonation* FLUENCY
- *Prefix* over- VOCABULARY STRATEGIES

Literature Discussion

You may want to call together small groups for literature discussion. See pp. 124–128 for suggested trade book titles.

Independent

Options for Independent Work

- Independent Reading
- Word Study
- Vocabulary in Context Cards 153–160
- Listening Center: respond in Reader's Notebook
- Reader's Notebook: see writing prompt
- Ready-Made Work Stations, Lesson 20: Comprehension and Fluency, Word Study, Think and Write

See Teacher's Edition Lesson 20 for more independent activity options.

Writing About Reading

- Prompt: In *Dex: The Heart of a Hero* and *Heroes Then and Now* you read about made-up and real-life heroes. Write about a time when someone you know acted like a hero. What did the person do? Why did it make him or her a hero?
- Have children use their Reader's Notebook to record reactions to the literature they read and listened to this week.

GROUP SHARE Wrap up each day's Readers' Workshop by asking children to share how they applied the minilesson principle to their independent reading. Look for the Group Share section at the end of each minilesson.

28 • Lesson 20

Suggested Weekly Focus

Lesson 21

Whole Group

Interactive Read-Aloud/Shared Reading

- *Penguin Chick* by Betty Tatham, Student Book: Lesson 21 NARRATIVE NONFICTION
- *From Duckling to Duck,* Teacher's Edition: Lesson 21 NARRATIVE NONFICTION
- *Animal Poems,* Student Book: Lesson 21 POETRY

Whole-Group Links

You may use the suggested links to teach and reinforce skills in shared reading.

- *r-Controlled Vowel* er PHONICS
- *r-Controlled Vowel* ir, ur PHONICS
- *Introduce Vocabulary (Vocabulary in Context Cards 161–168)* WORD STUDY
- *Dictionary Entry* VOCABULARY STRATEGIES

Reading Minilessons

- Main Idea and Details: Details About the Main Idea, p. 80
- Main Idea and Details: Details About the Main Idea, p. 81
- Genre: Poetry, p. 81

Use the minilessons in this guide as a bridge between shared reading experiences and guided/independent reading.

Small Group

Guided Reading

Select texts according to your children's instructional level. You may use the books below or select from the Leveled Readers Database, pp. 112–123. For instructional support, use the Leveled Readers Teacher's Guides along with the books that you choose.

- **LEVEL J**   *Penguins*   INFORMATIONAL TEXT
- **LEVEL L**   *Antarctic Animals* (Vocabulary Reader) INFORMATIONAL TEXT
- **LEVEL O**   *Going to the South Pole* (Language Support) INFORMATIONAL TEXT
- **LEVEL P**   *Exploring Antarctica*   INFORMATIONAL TEXT
- **LEVEL P**   *McMurdo Station*   INFORMATIONAL TEXT

For strategic intervention, use the Write-In Reader: *Joe and Trig and the Baby Turtles.*

Small-Group Links

- *Main Idea and Details; Infer/Predict* COMPREHENSION
- *r-Controlled Vowel* er PHONICS
- *r-Controlled Vowel* ir, ur PHONICS
- *Phrasing: Natural Pauses* FLUENCY
- *Dictionary Entry* VOCABULARY STRATEGIES

Literature Discussion

You may want to call together small groups for literature discussion. See pp. 124–128 for suggested trade book titles.

Independent

Options for Independent Work

- Independent Reading
- Word Study
- Vocabulary in Context Cards 161–168
- Listening Center: respond in Reader's Notebook
- Reader's Notebook: see writing prompt
- Ready-Made Work Stations, Lesson 21: Comprehension and Fluency, Word Study, Think and Write

See Teacher's Edition Lesson 21 for more independent activity options.

Writing About Reading

- Prompt: In *Penguin Chick,* you learned that penguins trumpet and whistle to communicate. Write a story about two penguins. Tell what they would say to each other if they could talk.
- Have children use their Reader's Notebook to record reactions to the literature they read and listened to this week.

GROUP SHARE Wrap up each day's Readers' Workshop by asking children to share how they applied the minilesson principle to their independent reading. Look for the Group Share section at the end of each minilesson.

Suggested Weekly Focus

Lesson 22

Whole Group

Interactive Read-Aloud/Shared Reading

- *Gloria Who Might Be My Best Friend* by Anne Cameron, Student Book: Lesson 22 REALISTIC FICTION
- *The Middle Seat,* Teacher's Edition: Lesson 22 REALISTIC FICTION
- *How to Make a Kite* by Joanna Korba, Student Book: Lesson 22 INFORMATIONAL TEXT

Whole-Group Links

You may use the suggested links to teach and reinforce skills in shared reading.

- *Homophones* PHONICS
- *Base Words and Endings* -er, -est PHONICS
- *Introduce Vocabulary (Vocabulary in Context Cards 169–176)* WORD STUDY
- *Figurative Language/Idioms* VOCABULARY STRATEGIES

Reading Minilessons

- Understanding Characters: How Characters Feel, p. 82
- Understanding Characters: What Characters Are Like, p. 83
- Genre: Informational Text, p. 83

Use the minilessons in this guide as a bridge between shared reading experiences and guided/independent reading.

Small Group

Guided Reading

Select texts according to your children's instructional level. You may use the books below or select from the Leveled Readers Database, pp. 112–123. For instructional support, use the Leveled Readers Teacher's Guides along with the books that you choose.

- **LEVEL I** *Friendship Rules!* (Vocabulary Reader) INFORMATIONAL TEXT
- **LEVEL I** *The Kite Contest* REALISTIC FICTION
- **LEVEL J** *Elena's Wish* (Language Support) REALISTIC FICTION
- **LEVEL K** *Every Kind of Wish* REALISTIC FICTION
- **LEVEL N** *Sand Castle Contest* REALISTIC FICTION

For strategic intervention, use the Write-In Reader: *Flood on River Road.*

Small-Group Links

- *Understanding Characters; Question* COMPREHENSION
- *Homophones* PHONICS
- *Base Words and Endings* -er, -est PHONICS
- *Accuracy: Self-Correct* FLUENCY
- *Figurative Language/Idioms* VOCABULARY STRATEGIES

Literature Discussion

You may want to call together small groups for literature discussion. See pp. 124–128 for suggested trade book titles.

Independent

Options for Independent Work

- Independent Reading
- Word Study
- Vocabulary in Context Cards 169–176
- Listening Center: respond in Reader's Notebook
- Reader's Notebook: see writing prompt
- Ready-Made Work Stations, Lesson 22: Comprehension and Fluency, Word Study, Think and Write

See Teacher's Edition Lesson 22 for more independent activity options.

Writing About Reading

- Prompt: In *How to Make a Kite,* the author gives instructions for making a kite. Think about something you know how to make. Write instructions to tell how to make it. Remember to write what you need to make it first.
- Have children use their Reader's Notebook to record reactions to the literature they read and listened to this week.

GROUP SHARE Wrap up each day's Readers' Workshop by asking children to share how they applied the minilesson principle to their independent reading. Look for the Group Share section at the end of each minilesson.

Suggested Weekly Focus

Lesson 23

Whole Group

Interactive Read-Aloud/ Shared Reading

- *The Goat in the Rug* by Charles L. Blood and Martin Link, Student Book: Lesson 23 NARRATIVE NONFICTION
- *Nothing But a Quilt,* Teacher's Edition: Lesson 23 INFORMATIONAL TEXT
- *Basket Weaving* by Becky Manfredini, Student Book: Lesson 23 INFORMATIONAL TEXT

Whole-Group Links

You may use the suggested links to teach and reinforce skills in shared reading.

- *Suffixes* -y, -ly, -ful PHONICS
- *Final Stable Syllables* -tion, -ture PHONICS
- *Introduce Vocabulary* (Vocabulary in Context Cards 177–184) WORD STUDY
- *Multiple-Meaning Words* VOCABULARY STRATEGIES

Reading Minilessons

- Conclusions: What Someone Is Like, p. 84
- Conclusions: What the Author Does Not Tell You, p. 85
- Text and Graphic Features: Special Ways the Author Shares Information, p. 85

Use the minilessons in this guide as a bridge between shared reading experiences and guided/independent reading.

Small Group

Guided Reading

Select texts according to your children's instructional level. You may use the books below or select from the Leveled Readers Database, pp. 112–123. For instructional support, use the Leveled Readers Teacher's Guides along with the books that you choose.

- **LEVEL J** *From Sheep to Sweater* INFORMATIONAL TEXT
- **LEVEL K** *Weaving* (Vocabulary Reader) INFORMATIONAL TEXT
- **LEVEL M** *How We Use Wool* (Language Support) INFORMATIONAL TEXT
- **LEVEL M** *Wool* INFORMATIONAL TEXT
- **LEVEL Q** *Textiles from Around the World* INFORMATIONAL TEXT

For strategic intervention, use the Write-In Reader: *I Made It Myself.*

Small-Group Links

- *Conclusions; Summarize* COMPREHENSION
- *Suffixes* -y, -ly, -ful PHONICS
- *Final Stable Syllables* -tion, -ture PHONICS
- *Rate: Adjust Rate to Purpose* FLUENCY
- *Multiple-Meaning Words* VOCABULARY STRATEGIES

Literature Discussion

You may want to call together small groups for literature discussion. See pp. 124–128 for suggested trade book titles.

Independent

Options for Independent Work

- Independent Reading
- Word Study
- Vocabulary in Context Cards 177–184
- Listening Center: respond in Reader's Notebook
- Reader's Notebook: see writing prompt
- Ready-Made Work Stations, Lesson 23: Comprehension and Fluency, Word Study, Think and Write

See Teacher's Edition Lesson 23 for more independent activity options.

Writing About Reading

- Prompt: In *The Goat in the Rug,* Geraldine tells the story. Think about how Glenmae might tell the story. Then write a part of the story the way Glenmae might tell it.
- Have children use their Reader's Notebook to record reactions to the literature they read and listened to this week.

GROUP SHARE Wrap up each day's Readers' Workshop by asking children to share how they applied the minilesson principle to their independent reading. Look for the Group Share section at the end of each minilesson.

Suggested Weekly Focus

Lesson 24

Whole Group

Interactive Read-Aloud/ Shared Reading

- *Half-Chicken* by Alma Flor Ada, Student Book: Lesson 24 FOLKTALE
- *Tiger in the Water: A Folktale from Malaysia,* Teacher's Edition: Lesson 24 FOLKTALE
- *The Lion and the Mouse,* Student Book: Lesson 24 FABLE

Whole-Group Links

You may use the suggested links to teach and reinforce skills in shared reading.

- *Prefixes* re-, un-, over-, pre-, mis- PHONICS
- *Silent Consonants* PHONICS
- *Introduce Vocabulary (Vocabulary in Context Cards 185–192)* WORD STUDY
- *Antonyms* VOCABULARY STRATEGIES

Reading Minilessons

- Cause and Effect: What Happens and Why, p. 86
- Cause and Effect: What Happens and Why, p. 87
- Genre: Fable, p. 87

Use the minilessons in this guide as a bridge between shared reading experiences and guided/independent reading.

Small Group

Guided Reading

Select texts according to your children's instructional level. You may use the books below or select from the Leveled Readers Database, pp. 112–123. For instructional support, use the Leveled Readers Teacher's Guides along with the books that you choose.

- **LEVEL J** *Clever Animals* (Vocabulary Reader) INFORMATIONAL TEXT
- **LEVEL J** *Favorite Fables* FABLE
- **LEVEL J** *The Trick* (Language Support) FOLKTALE
- **LEVEL M** *Coyote and Rabbit* FOLKTALE
- **LEVEL N** *Groundhog's New Home* FOLKTALE

For strategic intervention, use the Write-In Reader: *The Contest.*

Small-Group Links

- *Cause and Effect; Visualize* COMPREHENSION
- *Prefixes* re-, un-, over-, pre-, mis- PHONICS
- *Silent Consonants* PHONICS
- *Expression* FLUENCY
- *Antonyms* VOCABULARY STRATEGIES

Literature Discussion

You may want to call together small groups for literature discussion. See pp. 124–128 for suggested trade book titles.

Independent

Options for Independent Work

- Independent Reading
- Word Study
- Vocabulary in Context Cards 185–192
- Listening Center: respond in Reader's Notebook
- Reader's Notebook: see writing prompt
- Ready-Made Work Stations, Lesson 24: Comprehension and Fluency, Word Study, Think and Write

See Teacher's Edition Lesson 24 for more independent activity options.

Writing About Reading

- Prompt: In *The Lion and the Mouse,* the lion learns a lesson. Write your own story with a new character that learns the same lesson that the lion learns.
- Have children use their Reader's Notebook to record reactions to the literature they read and listened to this week.

GROUP SHARE Wrap up each day's Readers' Workshop by asking children to share how they applied the minilesson principle to their independent reading. Look for the Group Share section at the end of each minilesson.

Suggested Weekly Focus

Lesson 25

Whole Group

Interactive Read-Aloud/Shared Reading

- *How Groundhog's Garden Grew* by Lynne Cherry, Student Book: Lesson 25 FANTASY
- *An Apple a Day,* Teacher's Edition: Lesson 25 BIOGRAPHY
- *Super Soil,* Student Book: Lesson 25 INFORMATIONAL TEXT

Whole-Group Links

You may use the suggested links to teach and reinforce skills in shared reading.

- *Words with /aw/:* au, aw, al, o, a PHONICS
- *Introduce Vocabulary (Vocabulary in Context Cards 193–200)* WORD STUDY
- *Using Context* VOCABULARY STRATEGIES

Reading Minilessons

- Sequence of Events: Use the Order of Events to Understand What Happens, p. 88
- Sequence of Events: Use the Order of Events to Understand What Happens, p. 89
- Genre: Informational Text, p. 89

Use the minilessons in this guide as a bridge between shared reading experiences and guided/independent reading.

Small Group

Guided Reading

Select texts according to your children's instructional level. You may use the books below or select from the Leveled Readers Database, pp. 112–123. For instructional support, use the Leveled Readers Teacher's Guides along with the books that you choose.

- **LEVEL H** *The Giant Forest* FANTASY
- **LEVEL I** *Grow a Bean Plant!* (Vocabulary Reader) INFORMATIONAL TEXT
- **LEVEL L** *Rabbit's Garden* (Language Support) FANTASY
- **LEVEL L** *Rabbit's Garden Troubles* FANTASY
- **LEVEL N** *Bee's Beautiful Garden* FANTASY

For strategic intervention, use the Write-In Reader: *Daffodils.*

Small-Group Links

- *Sequence of Events; Monitor/Clarify* COMPREHENSION
- *Words with /aw/:* au, aw, al, o, a PHONICS
- *Phrasing: Punctuation* FLUENCY
- *Using Context* VOCABULARY STRATEGIES

Literature Discussion

You may want to call together small groups for literature discussion. See pp. 124–128 for suggested trade book titles.

Independent

Options for Independent Work

- Independent Reading
- Word Study
- Vocabulary in Context Cards 193–200
- Listening Center: respond in Reader's Notebook
- Reader's Notebook: see writing prompt
- Ready-Made Work Stations, Lesson 25: Comprehension and Fluency, Word Study, Think and Write

See Teacher's Edition Lesson 25 for more independent activity options.

Writing About Reading

- Prompt: In *How Groundhog's Garden Grew,* you read about the things Groundhog planted in his garden. Write about a garden you would like to plant. Tell what you would plant in your garden.
- Have children use their Reader's Notebook to record reactions to the literature they read and listened to this week.

GROUP SHARE Wrap up each day's Readers' Workshop by asking children to share how they applied the minilesson principle to their independent reading. Look for the Group Share section at the end of each minilesson.

Suggested Weekly Focus

Lesson 26

Whole Group

Interactive Read-Aloud/Shared Reading

- *The Mysterious Tadpole* by Steven Kellogg, Student Book: Lesson 26 FANTASY
- *Diego's Double Surprise,* Teacher's Edition: Lesson 26 REALISTIC FICTION
- *From Eggs to Frogs,* Student Book: Lesson 26 INFORMATIONAL TEXT

Whole-Group Links

You may use the suggested links to teach and reinforce skills in shared reading.

- *Words with* oo, ew, ue, ou PHONICS
- *Introduce Vocabulary (Vocabulary in Context Cards 201–208)* WORD STUDY
- *Multiple-Meaning Words* VOCABULARY STRATEGIES

Reading Minilessons

- Story Structure: How Setting Affects What Happens, p. 90
- Story Structure: Problem and Solution, p. 91
- Text and Graphic Features: Special Ways the Author Helps You Understand Ideas, p. 91

Use the minilessons in this guide as a bridge between shared reading experiences and guided/independent reading.

Small Group

Guided Reading

Select texts according to your children's instructional level. You may use the books below or select from the Leveled Readers Database, pp. 112–123. For instructional support, use the Leveled Readers Teacher's Guides along with the books that you choose.

- **LEVEL I**   *The Loch Ness Monster* (Vocabulary Reader) INFORMATIONAL TEXT
- **LEVEL J**   *Larry the Singing Chicken* FANTASY
- **LEVEL K**   *Jason and the Space Creature* (Language Support) FANTASY
- **LEVEL L**   *Planet Zogo* FANTASY
- **LEVEL N**   *Katy's Inventions* FANTASY

For strategic intervention, use the Write-In Reader: *Mr. Reed's Last Day.*

Small-Group Links

- *Story Structure; Infer/Predict* COMPREHENSION
- *Words with* oo, ew, ue, ou PHONICS
- *Accuracy: Connected Text* FLUENCY
- *Multiple-Meaning Words* VOCABULARY STRATEGIES

Literature Discussion

You may want to call together small groups for literature discussion. See pp. 124–128 for suggested trade book titles.

Independent

Options for Independent Work

- Independent Reading
- Word Study
- Vocabulary in Context Cards 201–208
- Listening Center: respond in Reader's Notebook
- Reader's Notebook: see writing prompt
- Ready-Made Work Stations, Lesson 26: Comprehension and Fluency, Word Study, Think and Write

See Teacher's Edition Lesson 26 for more independent activity options.

Writing About Reading

- Prompt: Imagine that Uncle McAllister from *The Mysterious Tadpole* gave you a gift from Scotland. Write him a thank-you note for the gift. Be sure to tell why you like it.
- Have children use their Reader's Notebook to record reactions to the literature they read and listened to this week.

GROUP SHARE Wrap up each day's Readers' Workshop by asking children to share how they applied the minilesson principle to their independent reading. Look for the Group Share section at the end of each minilesson.

Suggested Weekly Focus

Lesson 27

Whole Group

Interactive Read-Aloud/ Shared Reading

- *The Dog That Dug for Dinosaurs* by Shirley Raye Redmond, Student Book: Lesson 27 BIOGRAPHY
- *Epperson's Icicle,* Teacher's Edition: Lesson 27 INFORMATIONAL TEXT
- *La Brea Tar Pits* by Ciara McLaughlin, Student Book: Lesson 27 INFORMATIONAL TEXT

Whole-Group Links

You may use the suggested links to teach and reinforce skills in shared reading.

- *Words with* oo PHONICS
- *Possessive Nouns* PHONICS
- *Introduce Vocabulary (Vocabulary in Context Cards 209–216)* WORD STUDY
- *Synonyms* VOCABULARY STRATEGIES

Reading Minilessons

- Fact and Opinion: What Can Be Proved Versus What the Author Thinks, p. 92
- Genre: Informational Text, p. 93
- Text and Graphic Features: Time Line, p. 93

Use the minilessons in this guide as a bridge between shared reading experiences and guided/ independent reading.

Small Group

Guided Reading

Select texts according to your children's instructional level. You may use the books below or select from the Leveled Readers Database, pp. 112–123. For instructional support, use the Leveled Readers Teacher's Guides along with the books that you choose.

- **LEVEL I** *Dinosaur Fossils* (Vocabulary Reader) INFORMATIONAL TEXT
- **LEVEL L** *The Mysterious Bone* BIOGRAPHY
- **LEVEL L** *Sue Hendrickson: Fossil Hunter* (Language Support) BIOGRAPHY
- **LEVEL M** *Sue Hendrickson* BIOGRAPHY
- **LEVEL O** *Sir Hans Sloane* BIOGRAPHY

For strategic intervention, use the Write-In Reader: *Discovering the Past.*

Small-Group Links

- *Fact and Opinion; Question* COMPREHENSION
- *Words with* oo PHONICS
- *Possessive Nouns* PHONICS
- *Intonation* FLUENCY
- *Synonyms* VOCABULARY STRATEGIES

Literature Discussion

You may want to call together small groups for literature discussion. See pp. 124–128 for suggested trade book titles.

Independent

Options for Independent Work

- Independent Reading
- Word Study
- Vocabulary in Context Cards 209–216
- Listening Center: respond in Reader's Notebook
- Reader's Notebook: see writing prompt
- Ready-Made Work Stations, Lesson 27: Comprehension and Fluency, Word Study, Think and Write

See Teacher's Edition Lesson 27 for more independent activity options.

Writing About Reading

- Prompt: In *The Dog That Dug for Dinosaurs,* Mary and Tray find fossils near where they live. Write a story about a time when you found something at your home or in your neighborhood.
- Have children use their Reader's Notebook to record reactions to the literature they read and listened to this week.

GROUP SHARE Wrap up each day's Readers' Workshop by asking children to share how they applied the minilesson principle to their independent reading. Look for the Group Share section at the end of each minilesson.

Suggested Weekly Focus

Lesson 28

Whole Group

Interactive Read-Aloud/Shared Reading

- *Working in Space* by Patricia Whitehouse, Student Book: Lesson 28 INFORMATIONAL TEXT
- *Solving Problems with New Inventions,* Teacher's Edition: Lesson 28 INFORMATIONAL TEXT
- *Space Poems,* Student Book: Lesson 28 POETRY

Whole-Group Links

You may use the suggested links to teach and reinforce skills in shared reading.

- *Vowel Diphthongs* ow, ou PHONICS
- *Introduce Vocabulary* (Vocabulary in Context Cards 217–224) WORD STUDY
- *Classify/Categorize* VOCABULARY STRATEGIES

Reading Minilessons

- Text and Graphic Features: Special Ways the Author Helps You Understand Ideas, p. 94
- Compare and Contrast: How Things Are Alike and Different, p. 95
- Genre: Poetry, p. 95

Use the minilessons in this guide as a bridge between shared reading experiences and guided/independent reading.

Small Group

Guided Reading

Select texts according to your children's instructional level. You may use the books below or select from the Leveled Readers Database, pp. 112–123. For instructional support, use the Leveled Readers Teacher's Guides along with the books that you choose.

- **LEVEL I** *Staying Healthy in Space* INFORMATIONAL TEXT
- **LEVEL L** *Ready for Liftoff* (Vocabulary Reader) INFORMATIONAL TEXT
- **LEVEL M** *Trouble in Space* INFORMATIONAL TEXT
- **LEVEL M** *Trouble on a Trip to the Moon* (Language Support) INFORMATIONAL TEXT
- **LEVEL O** *The Red Planet* INFORMATIONAL TEXT

For strategic intervention, use the Write-In Reader: *Apollo 11: The Eagle Has Landed.*

Small-Group Links

- *Text and Graphic Features; Analyze/Evaluate* COMPREHENSION
- *Vowel Diphthongs* ow, ou PHONICS
- *Phrasing: Natural Pauses* FLUENCY
- *Classify/Categorize* VOCABULARY STRATEGIES

Literature Discussion

You may want to call together small groups for literature discussion. See pp. 124–128 for suggested trade book titles.

Independent

Options for Independent Work

- Independent Reading
- Word Study
- Vocabulary in Context Cards 217–224
- Listening Center: respond in Reader's Notebook
- Reader's Notebook: see writing prompt
- Ready-Made Work Stations, Lesson 28: Comprehension and Fluency, Word Study, Think and Write

See Teacher's Edition Lesson 28 for more independent activity options.

Writing About Reading

- Prompt: This week you read some poems about space. Write your own space poem about what you'd see if you were traveling through space.
- Have children use their Reader's Notebook to record reactions to the literature they read and listened to this week.

GROUP SHARE Wrap up each day's Readers' Workshop by asking children to share how they applied the minilesson principle to their independent reading. Look for the Group Share section at the end of each minilesson.

Suggested Weekly Focus

Lesson 29

Whole Group

Interactive Read-Aloud/Shared Reading

- *Two of Everything* by Lily Toy Hong, Student Book: Lesson 29 FOLKTALE
- *A Lesson in Happiness*, Teacher's Edition: Lesson 29 FOLKTALE
- *Stone Soup* adapted by Greta McLaughlin, Student Book: Lesson 29 FOLKTALE

Whole-Group Links

You may use the suggested links to teach and reinforce skills in shared reading.

- *Reading Longer Words* PHONICS
- *Vowel Diphthongs* oi, oy PHONICS
- *Introduce Vocabulary* (Vocabulary in Context Cards 225–232) WORD STUDY
- *Antonyms* VOCABULARY STRATEGIES

Reading Minilessons

- Understanding Characters: How Characters Change from Beginning to End, p. 96
- Understanding Characters: What Characters Are Like, p. 97
- Genre: Folktale, p. 97

Use the minilessons in this guide as a bridge between shared reading experiences and guided/independent reading.

Small Group

Guided Reading

Select texts according to your children's instructional level. You may use the books below or select from the Leveled Readers Database, pp. 112–123. For instructional support, use the Leveled Readers Teacher's Guides along with the books that you choose.

- **LEVEL I** *Brer Rabbit at the Well* FOLKTALE
- **LEVEL K** *The Smart Mouse* (Language Support) FOLKTALE
- **LEVEL L** *Mouse and Crocodile* FOLKTALE
- **LEVEL L** *Take a Trip to China* (Vocabulary Reader) INFORMATIONAL TEXT
- **LEVEL P** *Wali Dad's Gifts* FOLKTALE

For strategic intervention, use the Write-In Reader: *Fluff, Gus, and Bob*.

Small-Group Links

- *Understanding Characters; Summarize* COMPREHENSION
- *Reading Longer Words* PHONICS
- *Vowel Diphthongs* oi, oy PHONICS
- *Expression* FLUENCY
- *Antonyms* VOCABULARY STRATEGIES

Literature Discussion

You may want to call together small groups for literature discussion. See pp. 124–128 for suggested trade book titles.

Independent

Options for Independent Work

- Independent Reading
- Word Study
- Vocabulary in Context Cards 225–232
- Listening Center: respond in Reader's Notebook
- Reader's Notebook: see writing prompt
- Ready-Made Work Stations, Lesson 29: Comprehension and Fluency, Word Study, Think and Write

See Teacher's Edition Lesson 29 for more independent activity options.

Writing About Reading

- Prompt: *Stone Soup* is a folktale and also a play. Think of another folktale that could be performed as a play. Write part of the folktale as a play.
- Have children use their Reader's Notebook to record reactions to the literature they read and listened to this week.

GROUP SHARE Wrap up each day's Readers' Workshop by asking children to share how they applied the minilesson principle to their independent reading. Look for the Group Share section at the end of each minilesson.

Suggested Weekly Focus

Lesson 30

Whole Group

Interactive Read-Aloud/ Shared Reading

- *Now & Ben* by Gene Barretta, Student Book: Lesson 30 INFORMATIONAL TEXT
- *Godmothers and Goats,* Teacher's Edition: Lesson 30 INFORMATIONAL TEXT
- *A Model Citizen,* Student Book: Lesson 30 INFORMATIONAL TEXT

Whole-Group Links

You may use the suggested links to teach and reinforce skills in shared reading.

- *Reading Longer Words* PHONICS
- *Final Stable Syllable* -le PHONICS
- *Introduce Vocabulary* (Vocabulary in Context Cards 233–240) WORD STUDY
- *Dictionary* VOCABULARY STRATEGIES

Reading Minilessons

- Compare and Contrast: How Things Are Alike and Different, p. 98
- Compare and Contrast: How Things Are Alike and Different, p. 99
- Genre: Informational Text, p. 99

Use the minilessons in this guide as a bridge between shared reading experiences and guided/ independent reading.

Small Group

Guided Reading

Select texts according to your children's instructional level. You may use the books below or select from the Leveled Readers Database, pp. 112–123. For instructional support, use the Leveled Readers Teacher's Guides along with the books that you choose.

- **LEVEL M** *America's First Firefighters* INFORMATIONAL TEXT
- **LEVEL M** *Firefighters in America* (Language Support) INFORMATIONAL TEXT
- **LEVEL M** *Making a Newspaper* INFORMATIONAL TEXT
- **LEVEL M** *Philadelphia, 1756* (Vocabulary Reader) INFORMATIONAL TEXT
- **LEVEL Q** *From Trails to Highways* INFORMATIONAL TEXT

For strategic intervention, use the Write-In Reader: *Cyrus McCormick and His Reaper.*

Small-Group Links

- *Compare and Contrast; Visualize* COMPREHENSION
- *Reading Longer Words* PHONICS
- *Final Stable Syllable* -le PHONICS
- *Rate: Adjust Rate to Purpose* FLUENCY
- *Dictionary* VOCABULARY STRATEGIES

Literature Discussion

You may want to call together small groups for literature discussion. See pp. 124–128 for suggested trade book titles.

Independent

Options for Independent Work

- Independent Reading
- Word Study
- Vocabulary in Context Cards 233–240
- Listening Center: respond in Reader's Notebook
- Reader's Notebook: see writing prompt
- Ready-Made Work Stations, Lesson 30: Comprehension and Fluency, Word Study, Think and Write

See Teacher's Edition Lesson 30 for more independent activity options.

Writing About Reading

- Prompt: The author of *A Model Citizen* admires Ben Franklin for what he did. Write about a person you admire. What do you admire about him or her? What has he or she done?
- Have children use their Reader's Notebook to record reactions to the literature they read and listened to this week.

GROUP SHARE Wrap up each day's Readers' Workshop by asking children to share how they applied the minilesson principle to their independent reading. Look for the Group Share section at the end of each minilesson.

Whole-Group Lessons

Whole-group lessons provide a context for all children to think about what they read, learn from their peers' ideas, and demonstrate understanding of specific skills. To prepare for each lesson sequence on the pages that follow, we suggest that you:

- Read the literature in advance, and use self-stick notes to mark the suggested stopping points. As needed, supplement with questions that address your students' needs and allow for spontaneity of your students' responses.

- Set up an easel with chart paper (or use an overhead projector or whiteboard) to display minilesson principles and to share graphic organizers that you will complete with children.

Lesson 1	40	Lesson 16	70
Lesson 2	42	Lesson 17	72
Lesson 3	44	Lesson 18	74
Lesson 4	46	Lesson 19	76
Lesson 5	48	Lesson 20	78
Lesson 6	50	Lesson 21	80
Lesson 7	52	Lesson 22	82
Lesson 8	54	Lesson 23	84
Lesson 9	56	Lesson 24	86
Lesson 10	58	Lesson 25	88
Lesson 11	60	Lesson 26	90
Lesson 12	62	Lesson 27	92
Lesson 13	64	Lesson 28	94
Lesson 14	66	Lesson 29	96
Lesson 15	68	Lesson 30	98

Whole-Group Lessons

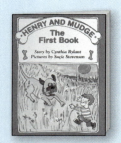

Henry and Mudge
Student Book, Lesson 1

The Perfect Pet
Teacher's Edition, Lesson 1

All in the Family
Student Book, Lesson 1

▶ Henry and Mudge

INTERACTIVE READ-ALOUD/SHARED READING

Read aloud the story to children. Stop periodically for very brief discussion of it. Use the following suggested stopping points and prompts for quick group response, or give a specific prompt and have partners or threes turn and talk.

- After Henry's parents agree to getting a dog, ask: "Why do Henry's parents agree to get Henry a dog? Turn and talk about your ideas with a partner."
- After Henry finds Mudge, ask: "Why did Henry choose Mudge over the other dogs he saw?"
- At the end of the story, ask: "Do you think Henry expected Mudge to grow so much? Why or why not?" Follow-up: "How do you think Henry and Mudge feel about each other? How do you know?"

MINILESSON Sequence of Events

TEACH Display the minilesson principle on chart paper, and read it aloud to children. Tell children they are going to think about what happens first, next, and last in a story. Explain that thinking about the story events in order will help them better understand the story.

1. Use *Henry and Mudge* to discuss the principle with children. Suggested language: "What happened first in the story *Henry and Mudge*?" *(Henry was lonely and wanted a dog.)* Point out that the author tells about Henry's problem first.
2. Guide children to think about which event happened next. Suggested language: "First, Henry was lonely and wanted a dog. What happened next?" *(He asked his parents for a dog and they agreed.)*
3. Guide children to think about what happened last. Suggested language: "First, Henry was lonely and wanted a dog. Next, he asked his parents for a dog and they agreed. What happened last, at the end of the story?" *(Henry found Mudge, who grew into a large dog.)*
4. Work with children to use their answers to the previous questions to tell what happened first, next, and last in the story. Record children's ideas in a Flow Chart like the one shown here.

> **MINILESSON PRINCIPLE**
>
> Notice how authors tell which story events happen first, next, and last.

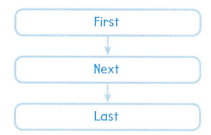

SUMMARIZE AND APPLY Restate the minilesson principle. Explain to children that they can apply it to their independent reading. Suggested language: "When you read a story, think about what happens first, next, and last."

GROUP SHARE Have children share stories they read for independent reading by telling what happened first, next, and last. Remind them to use the words *first, next,* and *last* to help tell the correct order of story events.

Lesson 1

▶ The Perfect Pet

INTERACTIVE READ-ALOUD/SHARED READING

Read aloud the story to children. Stop periodically for brief discussion of it. Use the following suggested stopping points and prompts:

- After Carla gives Sadie a big hug, ask: "How does Carla feel about Sadie? How do you know?"
- After Carla and her mother pet shop, ask: "Why doesn't Carla get a pet?" Follow-up: "What is the problem with each pet she sees?"
- At the end of the story, ask: "How does Carla solve both her problem and Mrs. Stevens's problem?" Follow-up: "What do you think will happen next? Turn and talk about your ideas with a partner."

MINILESSON Sequence of Events

TEACH Display the minilesson principle on chart paper, and read it aloud to children. Tell children that words such as *first, next, then,* and *last* will help them better understand the order of what happens in a story.

1. Reread the second paragraph of *The Perfect Pet* to children. Tell them to listen for the order in which things happen, and ask them to raise their hands when they hear the word *first, next, then,* or *last*.

> **MINILESSON PRINCIPLE**
>
> Notice how the words *first, next, then,* and *last* help you know the order of events.

2. Then help children retell the events from this paragraph in order. Suggested language: "What would Carla do first when she visited Sadie?" *(First, Carla would comb Sadie's fur.)* "What would Carla do next?" *(Next, Carla would take Sadie outside to play with her favorite string toy.)* Continue the same questioning pattern for *then* and *last*.

3. Point out to children that the words *first, next, then,* and *last* helped them figure out the order of story events. Ask volunteers to retell the events of the paragraph in order as you write them in a four-box Flow Chart labeled *First, Next, Then,* and *Last*. Have children use the time-order words.

SUMMARIZE AND APPLY Restate the minilesson principle. Tell children to apply it to their independent reading. Suggested language: "When you read, look for words such as *first, next, then,* and *last* to help you understand the order of events in a story."

GROUP SHARE Ask children to retell stories from independent reading using the words *first, next, then,* and *last* to tell about the order of story events.

▶ All in the Family

INTERACTIVE READ-ALOUD/SHARED READING

Read aloud the book to children. Stop periodically for brief discussion. Use the following suggested stopping points and prompts:

- After the author tells about dogs, ask: "How are wild dogs and pet dogs the same? How are they different?"
- At the end, say: "Each section in this book follows a pattern. What is the pattern?" Follow-up: "How does the pattern help you understand the book? Turn and talk about your ideas with a partner."

MINILESSON Genre: Informational Text

TEACH Tell children they are going to think about the information the author tells in *All in the Family*.

1. Discuss the principle with children, using *All in the Family* as an example. Suggested language: "There are different kinds of books. Some books tell stories. Other books give information or tell about facts. What kind of book is *All in the Family*?" *(an informational book)* Follow-up: "How do you know?" *(It gives information and facts about zoo animals and pets that are in the same animal family.)*

> **MINILESSON PRINCIPLE**
>
> Think about the information the author tells.

2. Ask children to share the information from *All in the Family*. Suggested language: "What information do you remember from *All in the Family*?" *(Answers will vary.)* Follow-up: "What information did you think was most interesting? Why?" *(Answers will vary.)*

3. Guide children to tell about groups of animals they learned about in *All in the Family*. Then write the minilesson principle on chart paper, and read it aloud. Explain to children that thinking about the information the author tells will help them learn things from an informational book.

SUMMARIZE AND APPLY Restate the minilesson principle. Tell children to apply it to their independent reading. Suggested language: "When you read informational books, think about the information the author tells."

GROUP SHARE Ask children to share some information from an informational book that they read for independent reading.

Whole-Group Lessons • **41**

Whole-Group Lessons

My Family
Student Book, Lesson 2

More Than a Best Friend
Teacher's Edition, Lesson 2

Family Poetry
Student Book, Lesson 2

▶ **My Family**

INTERACTIVE READ-ALOUD/SHARED READING

Read the book aloud to children. Stop periodically to discuss it very briefly. Use the following suggested stopping points and prompts for quick group response, or give a specific prompt and have partners or threes turn and talk.

- After the section about Camila's grandmother coming to visit, ask: "What are some of the things you learn about Camila on these pages?"
- After the section that shows the family tree, ask: "Who are some of the family members who came to René's birthday party?" Follow-up: "Why do you think the diagram of Camila's family is included in this book?"
- After the section about Sundays, ask: "Why is Sunday important to Camila and her family? Turn and talk about your ideas with a partner."
- At the end, ask: "Why do you think Camila likes fishing with her Papi best?"

MINILESSON Compare and Contrast

TEACH Display the minilesson principle on chart paper, and read it aloud to children. Tell children they are going to learn to think about how the things they read about are the same and how they are different.

1. Discuss the principle with children, using *My Family* as an example. Suggested language: "In *My Family*, you learned about Camila's family. Who is part of Camila's family?" *(Camila has a mother, a father, a brother, and many other family members.)* Follow-up: "What do they like to do?" *(They have birthday parties and get together on Sundays to play music.)*

2. Help children compare Camila's family to other families. Suggested language: "What are some of the ways in which Camila's family is the same as other families you know?" *(They are the same because many families have different family members who like to do things together.)*

3. Have children contrast Camila's family with other families. Suggested language: "How may Camila's family be different from other families?" *(Possible responses: Camila's family has many family members. Other families may have only a few people. Camila's family likes to play music together. Other families may enjoy doing other things.)*

4. Work with children to tell ways that Camila's family is the same as and different from other families. Record children's ideas in a Venn Diagram like the one shown here.

> **MINILESSON PRINCIPLE**
>
> Think about how things are the same and how they are different.

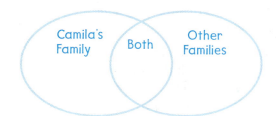

SUMMARIZE AND APPLY Restate the minilesson principle. Explain to children that they can apply it to their independent reading. Suggested language: "When you read a book, think about how the things you read about are the same and how they are different."

GROUP SHARE Have children tell about how two characters, places, or things in a book they read were the same and how they were different.

42 • Lesson 2

Lesson 2

▶ More Than a Best Friend

INTERACTIVE READ-ALOUD/SHARED READING

Read aloud the selection to children. Stop periodically for brief discussion of it. Use the following suggested stopping points and prompts:

- After the second paragraph, ask: "Why might a person who cannot see want a guide dog?"
- After reading about Mary and her guide dog, ask: "Why do you think guide dogs become close friends of their owners?"
- At the end, ask: "How do hearing dogs help people who cannot hear?" Follow-up: "Why do you think the author wrote this story? Turn and talk about your ideas with a partner."

MINILESSON Compare and Contrast

TEACH Display the minilesson principle on chart paper, and read it aloud to children. Tell children they will learn to think about how things are the same and how they are different.

1. Discuss the principle with children, using *More Than a Best Friend* as an example. Suggested language: "In *More Than a Best Friend*, you learned about guide dogs and hearing dogs. What kinds of things do they each do?" *(Guide dogs help blind people do things such as cross the street. Hearing dogs help deaf people know when the phone is ringing.)*

> **MINILESSON PRINCIPLE**
>
> Think about how things are the same and how they are different.

2. Help children tell how guide dogs and pet dogs are the same. Suggested language: "What is the same about guide dogs and pet dogs?" *(They are the same because they are smart, loyal, and helpful.)*

3. Have children tell how guide dogs and pet dogs are different. Suggested language: "How are guide dogs different from pet dogs?" *(Guide dogs have jobs to do, such as helping blind people cross streets and other things. Pet dogs do not have jobs to do.)*

4. Work with children to compare and contrast guide dogs and pet dogs. Record children's ideas in a Venn Diagram labeled *Guide Dogs, Both,* and *Pet Dogs.*

SUMMARIZE AND APPLY Restate the minilesson principle. Explain to children that they should apply it to their independent reading. Suggested language: "When you read, think about how things are the same and how they are different."

GROUP SHARE Have children tell how two people, animals, or events are the same and different in a book they are reading.

▶ Family Poetry

INTERACTIVE READ-ALOUD/SHARED READING

Read aloud the introduction and poems to children. Stop periodically for brief discussion of the poems. Use the following suggested stopping points and prompts:

- After the poem "Everybody Says," ask: "What is the problem that the poet describes?" Follow-up: "Have you ever felt the same way? Turn and talk about your ideas with a partner."
- After the poem "Abuelita's Lap," ask: "How does each section of the poem begin?" Follow-up: "What place is the speaker talking about?"

MINILESSON Genre: Poetry

TEACH Remind children that they have read three poems: "Everybody Says," "Abuelita's Lap," and "What Is a Family?" Explain to children that some poems have words that show feeling.

1. Read aloud the last line of "Everybody Says," emphasizing the words *I* and *me*. Ask: "How do you think the poet feels about looking like herself?" *(She feels strongly about wanting to look like herself, not someone else.)*

> **MINILESSON PRINCIPLE**
>
> Notice that some poems have words that show feeling.

2. Point out to children the slanted type of *I*, the capital letters of *ME*, and the exclamation mark at the end. Ask: "How did the special type help you know how the girl felt?" *(They showed which words were important to her and how strongly she felt.)*

3. Help children notice words that show feelings in the other poems. Prompt children to recognize the words in the poem that helped create these feelings as you write the minilesson principle on chart paper. Explain to children that thinking about the words that show feeling in poems will help them enjoy them more.

SUMMARIZE AND APPLY Restate the minilesson principle. Tell children to apply it to their independent reading. Suggested language: "When you read poems, think about how the words show feeling."

GROUP SHARE Ask children to share poems that they especially enjoyed and the words from those poems that showed feeling. Have them explain how these words helped them understand the poem.

Whole-Group Lessons • 43

Whole-Group Lessons

Henry and Mudge Under the Yellow Moon
Student Book, Lesson 3

The Owl Hunt
Teacher's Edition, Lesson 3

Outdoor Adventures
Student Book, Lesson 3

▶ **Henry and Mudge Under the Yellow Moon**

INTERACTIVE READ-ALOUD/SHARED READING

Read aloud the story to children. Stop periodically to discuss it very briefly. Use the following suggested stopping points and prompts for quick group response, or give a specific prompt and have partners or threes turn and talk.

- After Mudge eats a few leaves, ask: "What do Henry and Mudge both like in the fall?" Follow-up: "How do they show this in different ways?"
- After Henry and Mudge watch birds and chipmunks, ask: "Why are the birds flying south?" Follow-up: "Why do you think the chipmunks are busy?"
- At the end of the story, ask: "What is this story mostly about? Turn and talk with a partner about your ideas."

MINILESSON Author's Purpose

TEACH Display the minilesson principle on chart paper, and read it aloud to children. Tell children they are going to think about how the author, Cynthia Rylant, wrote this story for readers to enjoy.

1. Use *Henry and Mudge Under the Yellow Moon* to discuss the principle with children. Suggested language: "There are different kinds of books. Some books give information or tell about real things. Some books tell stories. What kind of book is *Henry and Mudge Under the Yellow Moon*?" (a story book) Follow-up: "How do you know?" (*It tells a made-up story about the made-up characters Henry and Mudge.*)

2. Reread the sentence, *Henry picked apples and Mudge licked apples*. Ask: "Why was this sentence fun to read?" (*It was silly when Mudge licked the apples.*) Then ask: "Why do you think the author made this sentence fun to read?" (*She wanted to help her readers enjoy the story.*)

3. Repeat the procedure and the questioning with the two sentences on page 75. Then guide children to understand why the author wrote the story. Say: "Think about what you just read and what you learned. Why do you think Cynthia Rylant wrote this story?" (*She wanted to give readers something fun to read.*)

4. Work with children to use their answers to the previous questions to tell how the author wrote to help readers enjoy the story. Have children share pages or events from the story that were fun to read. Record their responses in an Inference Map like the one shown here.

> **MINILESSON PRINCIPLE**
> Think about how authors sometimes write to help readers enjoy their stories.

SUMMARIZE AND APPLY Restate the minilesson principle. Then tell children to apply it to their independent reading. Suggested language: "When you read a book, think about how the author wrote to help you enjoy the story."

GROUP SHARE Have children share whether the book they are reading independently was written for readers to enjoy. Ask them to tell how the author helped them enjoy the book.

44 • Lesson 3

Lesson 3

▶ The Owl Hunt

INTERACTIVE READ-ALOUD/SHARED READING

Read aloud the story to children. Stop periodically to discuss it briefly. Use the following suggested stopping points and prompts:

- After Sylvester eats a spider, ask: "What is happening in the beginning of this story?"
- After Macy and Sylvester decide to fly south, ask: "What are Macy and Sylvester learning in school?" Follow-up: "Why is this especially important for an owl to learn?"
- At the end of the story, say: "Why does Macy think the black dome may be a monster?" Follow-up: "What does the dome turn out to be?"

MINILESSON Genre: Fantasy

TEACH Display the minilesson principle on chart paper, and read it aloud to children. Explain that noticing which parts of a story are make-believe and which could happen in real life will help them better understand a story.

1. Explain to children that there are different kinds of stories. Tell them that in some stories the characters seem like real people, and what happens could happen in real life. Point out that in other stories the characters could not be real, and the things that happen are make-believe.

> **MINILESSON PRINCIPLE**
>
> Notice which parts of the story are make-believe.

2. Then help children recall the characters in *The Owl Hunt*. Suggested language: "Who was the main character in *The Owl Hunt*?" (*Macy Owl*) "Who are Macy and Sylvester?" (*They are young owls.*) "Are Macy and Sylvester real or make-believe?" (*make-believe*) "How do you know?" (*Possible answer: Macy is an owl that talks and goes to owl school. This cannot happen in real life.*)

3. Ask children to identify other characters and things that happen in the story that are make-believe and explain why. Write these story details in a T-Map labeled *Character or What Happens* and *Why It Is Make-Believe*.

SUMMARIZE AND APPLY Restate the minilesson principle. Tell children to apply it to their independent reading. Suggested language: "When you read a story, look for parts that are make-believe."

GROUP SHARE Ask children to tell about stories from independent reading, and have them describe parts that are make-believe.

▶ Outdoor Adventures

INTERACTIVE READ-ALOUD/SHARED READING

Read aloud the introduction and e-mails to children. Stop periodically to discuss the e-mails briefly. Use the following suggested stopping points and prompts:

- After the e-mail from Lola, ask: "Who is the e-mail from? Who is the e-mail to?" Follow-up: "What can you tell about Lola from her e-mail?"
- At the end of the selection, ask: "How are the e-mails the same? How are they different? Turn and talk about your ideas with a partner."

MINILESSON Text and Graphic Features

TEACH Tell children they are going to think about some ways they got information in *Outdoor Adventures*.

1. Discuss the principle with children, using *Outdoor Adventures* as an example. Suggested language: "Look at the photo in Lola's e-mail. What do you see?" (*geese flying*) Follow-up: "Look at the words in dark type below the photo. What extra information did you get from reading these words?" (*Geese fly in a V shape. They take turns flying in the front because it helps them fly longer.*)

> **MINILESSON PRINCIPLE**
>
> Think about how the pictures and labels give you information.

2. Ask children to describe the pictures and labels on the next page. Then discuss their purpose. Suggested language: "Why do you think the author used photos and the labels below them?" (*They help show extra information that the e-mail does not give. They explain the photos and help you understand what the photos show.*)

3. Write the minilesson principle on chart paper. Explain to children that thinking about the information in the pictures and labels will help them better understand what they read in books that give information. Help children to summarize what they learned from the pictures and labels in *Outdoor Adventures*. Use their ideas to fill in a T-Map with the headings *Picture and Label* and *Information They Tell*.

SUMMARIZE AND APPLY Restate the minilesson principle. Tell children to apply it to their independent reading. Suggested language: "When you read information books, be sure to look at the pictures and read the labels to get more information."

GROUP SHARE Ask children to share some information from a photo and label in an information book that they read for independent reading.

Whole-Group Lessons • 45

Whole-Group Lessons

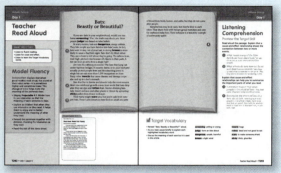

Diary of a Spider
Student Book, Lesson 4

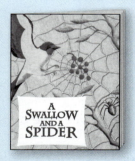

Bats: Beastly or Beautiful?
Teacher's Edition, Lesson 4

A Swallow and a Spider
Student Book, Lesson 4

▶ Diary of a Spider

INTERACTIVE READ-ALOUD/SHARED READING

Read aloud the story to children. Stop periodically to discuss it briefly. Use the following suggested stopping points and prompts for quick group response, or give a specific prompt and have partners or threes turn and talk.

- After the March 29th entry, ask: "What is special about the way the author is telling this story?" Follow-up: "How does it help you understand what is happening?"
- After the April 12th entry, ask: "What did Spider learn at Safety Day? How is this like what you have learned to do in the case of a fire? Turn and talk about your ideas with a partner."
- After the July 9th entry, ask: "How do Spider and his Grampa feel about each other?" Follow-up: "What clues from the story help you understand how they feel?"
- At the end of the story, ask: "Why do you think the author wrote this story? Talk about your ideas with a partner."

MINILESSON Cause and Effect

TEACH Display the minilesson principle on chart paper, and read it aloud to children. Tell children they are going to learn to think about what happens and why it happens as they read. Point out that understanding how one event makes another event happen will help them better understand the story.

1. Discuss the principle with children, using examples from *Diary of a Spider*. Help children recognize how one event can make another event happen. Suggested language: "When Spider and his sister went to the park, they spun a web on the water fountain. How did this event make another event happen?" *(A girl got stuck on the web.)*

2. Help children identify another event from the story. Suggested language: "On June 5, Fly wouldn't come out of her tree house. What made this event happen?" *(Daddy Longlegs had made fun of Fly.)*

3. Help children identify more events that cause other events to happen. Suggested language: "On June 7, Grampa blew away in the wind. What happened to Grampa?" *(He blew away.)* "What made this happen?" *(the wind)*

4. Use children's answers to the above questions to record selected events from the story and what made them happen. Record children's ideas in a T-Map like the one shown here.

> **MINILESSON PRINCIPLE**
> Notice when one event makes another event happen.

What Happened	What Made It Happen

SUMMARIZE AND APPLY Restate the minilesson principle. Then tell children to apply it to their independent reading. Suggested language: "When you read, think about how one event makes another event happen."

GROUP SHARE Ask children to share an event from a story they read for independent reading and explain what made that event happen.

46 • Lesson 4

Lesson 4

▶ Bats: Beastly or Beautiful?

INTERACTIVE READ-ALOUD/SHARED READING

Read the passage aloud to children. Stop periodically to discuss it briefly. Use the following suggested stopping points and prompts:

- After reading the second paragraph, ask: "Why do some people think that bats would fly into their hair?" Follow-up: "Why won't this happen?"
- After reading the third paragraph, ask: "How do bats help protect people from mosquitoes and other insects?"
- At the end of the passage, ask: "How does the author feel about vampire bats?" Follow-up: "Do you agree with the author? Turn and talk about your ideas with a partner."

MINILESSON Cause and Effect

TEACH Display the minilesson principle on chart paper, and read it aloud to children. Tell children that they will learn more about how to notice when one event (the cause) makes another event happen (the effect).

1. Help children identify a cause and its effect from *Bats: Beastly or Beautiful?* Suggested language: "The author says that people judge bats based on false beliefs. What do people do?" *(They judge bats.)* "What makes people judge bats?" *(false beliefs)* Point out that one thing makes another thing happen.

> **MINILESSON PRINCIPLE**
>
> Notice when one event makes another event happen.

2. Help children to identify another event or idea from the passage. Suggested language: "You learned that many people have the wrong idea about bats. What is something that makes this happen?"*(Possible answer: Movies show bats as dangerous, creepy critters.)*

3. Tell children to think about how these ideas are connected. Suggested language: "People judge bats because they have seen movies that show bats as dangerous, creepy critters."

4. Help children identify additional events or ideas from the passage. Record their ideas in a T-Map labeled *What Happened* and *What Made It Happen*.

SUMMARIZE AND APPLY Restate the minilesson principle. Then tell children to apply it to their independent reading. Suggested language: "When you read, notice the events that make other events happen."

GROUP SHARE Ask children to share an event from a book they read and tell what made it happen.

▶ A Swallow and a Spider

INTERACTIVE READ-ALOUD/SHARED READING

Read aloud the play to children. Stop periodically for brief discussion of it. Use the following suggested stopping points and prompts:

- After the first page, ask: "What do you think is the same about Spider and Swallow?" *(They both want to eat.)* Follow-up: "What do you think will happen next?"
- After the second page, ask: "Why does Spider want to catch Swallow?" Follow-up: "Do you think Spider's plan will work? Turn and talk about your ideas with a partner."
- At the end of the play, ask: "Why do you think Spider told Swallow that the berries were rotten?"

MINILESSON Genre: Fable

TEACH Explain to children that *A Swallow and a Spider* is a fable, or a story in which a character learns a lesson. Tell children they will learn to think about the lesson that the author is trying to teach.

1. Focus on *A Swallow and a Spider* to discuss the idea that a fable is a story that teaches a lesson. Suggested language: "In the story *A Swallow and a Spider*, Spider learned a lesson. Why did Spider want to catch Swallow in her web?" *(because Swallow ate flies that Spider wanted)* "What happened when Swallow flew to the web to get the berries?" *(He flew right through the web.)* Follow-up: "What did Spider learn?" *(She learned that she is not a bird-catcher, and she should stick to what she knows how to do.)*

> **MINILESSON PRINCIPLE**
>
> Think about what lesson the author is trying to teach.

2. Explain that sometimes in a fable, the author writes the lesson at the end of the story. Guide children to reread the moral of the story at the end of *A Swallow and a Spider*.

3. Guide children to explain the lesson of the story as you write the minilesson principle on chart paper. Explain to children that knowing what to expect when they read a fable will help them understand the lesson the author is trying to teach.

SUMMARIZE AND APPLY Restate the minilesson principle. Tell children to apply it to their independent reading. Suggested language: "When you read, look for a lesson that the story teaches."

GROUP SHARE Ask children to explain a lesson in a fable or other story they read for independent reading.

Whole-Group Lessons • **47**

Whole-Group Lessons

Teacher's Pets
Student Book, Lesson 5

Lester
Teacher's Edition, Lesson 5

See Westburg by Bus!
Student Book, Lesson 5

▶ Teacher's Pets

INTERACTIVE READ-ALOUD/SHARED READING

Read aloud the story to children. Stop periodically for very brief discussion of it. Use the following suggested stopping points and prompts for quick group response, or give a specific prompt and have partners or threes turn and talk.

- After the first page, ask: "Why does Miss Fry tell Winston that he can only bring his pet in for the day?" Follow-up: "Why might she not want pets to stay overnight?"
- After Miss Fry feeds Red and Vincent, ask: "Do you notice a pattern to the story?" Follow-up: "What do you think might happen next?"
- Show children the picture of Miss Fry's classroom door with the noises coming from it and ask: "Why do you think the illustrator only shows the classroom door in this picture instead of the inside?" Follow-up: "What do you picture in your mind about what is happening behind the door?"
- At the end of the story, ask: "How do you think Miss Fry feels about having Moe as her pet?"

MINILESSON Story Structure

TEACH Display the minilesson principle on chart paper, and read it aloud to children. Tell children they are going to learn to think about the important events in a story.

1. Discuss the principle with children, using an example from *Teacher's Pets*. Suggested language: "In *Teacher's Pets*, Winston asked Miss Fry if he could bring a pet for sharing day. Why is that an important event?" *(It is important because he started the pattern of bringing pets to class and then leaving them there.)*

2. Focus on the pages that show when the rest of the class brings in pets. Suggested language: "Why is it important that many children bring pets into class?" *(It is important because if it were just one pet in the classroom, it wouldn't be such a problem.)*

3. Use children's responses to display and complete a Flow Chart that shows the important events in the story.

> **MINILESSON PRINCIPLE**
> Think about the important events in the story.

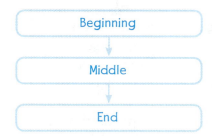

SUMMARIZE AND APPLY Restate the minilesson principle. Then tell children to apply it to their independent reading. Suggested language: "When you read, think about the important events in the story."

GROUP SHARE Ask children to share the important events in a story from their independent reading.

Lesson 5

▶ Lester

INTERACTIVE READ-ALOUD/SHARED READING

Read aloud the story to children. Stop periodically for brief discussion of it. Use the following suggested stopping points and prompts:

- After the first paragraph, ask: "Why do you think Lester is the class's favorite pet?"
- After the children call out their ideas for finding Lester, say: "Think about a time when you lost something you cared about. Turn and talk with your partner about what you did to find it."
- At the end of the story, ask: "Why did Lester leave his cage?"

MINILESSON Story Structure

TEACH Display the minilesson principle on chart paper, and read it aloud to children. Tell children they are going to learn to think about what the problem in a story is.

1. Ask children to think about what happened in the story *Lester*. Suggested language: "In the story *Lester*, we read about Mrs. Carpenter's class, which had a lot of class pets. What happened to one of these pets?" *(The class's favorite pet, Lester, went missing.)*

> **MINILESSON PRINCIPLE**
>
> Think about what the problem in a story is.

2. Guide children to understand that this event—the fact that Lester is missing—is the problem in the story. Suggested language: "Most stories have a problem that must be solved. What was the problem in this story?" *(Lester was missing from his cage.)* Follow-up: "How was that problem solved?" *(Lester returned to his cage with a friend.)*

3. Discuss with children that most story problems have a solution. Explain that the problem and solution of a story are what make up the story's plot. Guide them to discuss the story *Lester*. Use their ideas to complete a Story Map on chart paper.

SUMMARIZE AND APPLY Restate the minilesson principle. Tell children to apply it to their independent reading. Suggested language: "When you read, think about what the problem in the story is."

GROUP SHARE Ask children to share an example of a problem from a story that they read in independent reading.

▶ See Westburg by Bus!

INTERACTIVE READ-ALOUD/SHARED READING

Read aloud the book to children. Stop periodically for brief discussion of it. Use the following suggested stopping points and prompts:

- After the first page, ask: "What is a Welcome Center? What things might you find at a Welcome Center?"
- At the end, ask: "What is your favorite place in your town? Turn and talk with a partner about why you like to visit your favorite place."

MINILESSON Genre: Informational Text

TEACH Explain to children that *See Westburg by Bus!* is different from the other two stories they read this week because it is an information book. Tell children that they will learn to think about how the author tells information in order.

1. Talk about the title and the first paragraph to help children identify the topic. Suggested language: "The title, *See Westburg by Bus!*, and the first paragraph tell you that you will read about the places in the town of Westburg. One sentence also tells you to follow the numbers on the map."

> **MINILESSON PRINCIPLE**
>
> Think about how the author tells steps in order.

2. Page through the book with children, pointing out how the numbers on the map match the words about each place. Suggested language: "You started by looking for step number 1. When you found the location on the map, you saw that the first stop was the Welcome Center. Then you read the paragraph that went with it. What was at that next step?" *(the library)*

3. Write the minilesson principle on chart paper, and read it aloud. Guide children to follow the tour steps in order. Help them realize that the author gave numbers so that the tour through Westburg could be followed in an order that made sense.

SUMMARIZE AND APPLY Restate the minilesson principle. Tell children to apply it to their independent reading. Suggested language: "When you read an information book, think about how the author tells steps in order."

GROUP SHARE Ask children to share examples of how the author told steps in order in a book they chose for independent reading.

Whole-Group Lessons • **49**

Whole-Group Lessons

Animals Building Homes
Student Book, Lesson 6

City Life Is for the Birds
Teacher's Edition, Lesson 6

Hiding at the Pond
Student Book, Lesson 6

▶ Animals Building Homes

INTERACTIVE READ-ALOUD/SHARED READING

Read aloud the book to children. Stop periodically for very brief discussion of it. Use the following suggested stopping points and prompts for quick group response, or give a specific prompt and have partners or threes turn and talk.

- After you read the section called Safe at Home, ask: "What are some reasons animals build homes? Turn and talk about it with a partner."
- After you read the section called Careful Builders, ask: "What animal did you learn about in this section? What did you learn about it?"
- After you read Working Together, ask: "What is the title of this section? What does the title have to do with the information in the section?"
- At the end of the book, ask: "Which animal home did you find most interesting? Why?"

MINILESSON Text and Graphic Features

TEACH Display the minilesson principle on chart paper, and read it aloud to children. Tell children they are going to learn how to use pictures to understand the words in a book they are reading. Point out that this will help them understand what the book is about.

1. Discuss the principle with children, using examples from *Animals Building Homes*. Suggested language: "In *Animals Building Homes*, you saw pictures of animal homes. How did the pictures help you understand how the homes can be different?" *(The pictures showed that some homes are nests, while others are burrows or holes that the animals dug.)*

2. Focus on the picture of foxes in a hole at the beginning of the book. Suggested language: "Look at the picture of the foxes in the section Safe at Home. How does the picture tell about those words?" *(The picture shows foxes in a hole, perhaps trying to stay safe from a bigger animal. This helps me understand what Safe at Home will be about; the section is about how animals use their homes to stay safe.)*

3. Continue asking questions about other photographs in the book. Use children's responses to fill in a T-Map like the one shown here.

MINILESSON PRINCIPLE

Notice how you can look at the pictures to understand the words.

Picture	What It Tells Me

SUMMARIZE AND APPLY Restate the minilesson principle. Then tell children to apply it to their independent reading. Suggested language: "When you read, think about how you can use pictures to understand the words you are reading."

GROUP SHARE Ask children to tell how pictures helped them understand the books they read for independent reading.

50 • Lesson 6

Lesson 6

▶ City Life Is for the Birds

INTERACTIVE READ-ALOUD/SHARED READING

Read aloud the story to children. Stop periodically for brief discussion of it. Use the following suggested stopping points and prompts:

- After the people decide to get rid of the nest, ask: "What big problem do Pale Male and Lola have?"
- After the birds try to rebuild the nest, ask: "Why are the bird lovers angry?" Follow-up: "What do they want the people who live in the apartment building to do?"
- At the end, ask: "How do you think you would have felt if you lived in the apartment building?" Follow-up: "What would you have done? Turn and talk about your ideas with a partner."

MINILESSON Genre: Informational Text

TEACH Display the minilesson principle on chart paper, and read it aloud to children. Tell children they are going to learn about how authors make facts and information interesting.

1. Discuss with children some of the facts they learned about the hawks from this story. Suggested language: "What did you learn about where red-tailed hawks can live and how they build their nests?" *(Possible answers: They live high in trees or buildings. They make their nests out of sticks and twigs.)*

> **MINILESSON PRINCIPLE**
>
> Notice how the author makes information interesting.

2. Next, guide children to discuss the parts of the story they thought were most fun or interesting. Ask: "What did you like about how the author wrote this story?" *(Possible answer: I liked how the author gave details about the mess the hawks made in front of the apartment building. I liked how I could picture what was happening.)*

3. Use children's responses to focus on how the author made these facts more interesting by writing a story about two real birds. Ask: "How did learning about Pale Male and Lola help you understand the important information about hawks?" *(It helped me understand that the hawks probably did not want to move, so I was more interested in how the story would end. It made me want to learn more about hawks.)*

SUMMARIZE AND APPLY Restate the minilesson principle. Tell children to apply it to their independent reading. Suggested language: "When you read, think about how authors make information interesting."

GROUP SHARE Have children share information they learned in books they have read and how the authors made this information fun to read about.

▶ Hiding at the Pond

INTERACTIVE READ-ALOUD/SHARED READING

Read aloud the play to children. Stop periodically for brief discussion of it. Use the following suggested stopping points and prompts:

- After Bullfrog meets Walking Stick, ask: "Where does this story take place? How do you know?"
- At the end of the play, ask: "Why didn't Bullfrog see Walking Stick and Snapping Turtle at first?"

MINILESSON Genre: Play

TEACH Write the minilesson principle on chart paper, and read it aloud to children. Explain to children that *Hiding at the Pond* is a special kind of story that is different from many other stories they have read because it is a play.

1. Focus on *Hiding at the Pond* to introduce the idea that in a play, the characters' words tell the story. Suggested language: "The play *Hiding at the Pond* has three characters: Bullfrog, Walking Stick, and Snapping Turtle. These characters' words told the whole story. How could you tell who was speaking?" *(A character's name was in front of each thing that was said.)*

> **MINILESSON PRINCIPLE**
>
> Notice that the characters' words tell the story in a play.

2. Guide children to use the characters' words to figure out what happened in the story. Suggested language: "Think about Bullfrog's words *I'll hop along this winding path around the pond*. What did these words tell you about the story?" *(The story took place at a pond. Frog was hopping along.)* Guide children to use other words to tell what the characters were doing in the play. Then have them use this information to tell what the play was about. Explain to children that they will better understand plays if they pay attention to characters' words for clues about the story.

SUMMARIZE AND APPLY Restate the minilesson principle. Tell children to apply it to their independent reading. Suggested language: "When you read a play, pay attention to characters' words to figure out what is happening in the story."

GROUP SHARE Ask children to tell how characters' words helped them understand the events in stories they read for independent reading.

Whole-Group Lessons • 51

Whole-Group Lessons

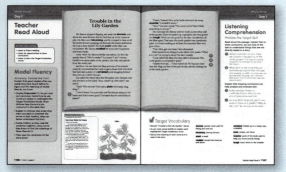

The Ugly Vegetables
Student Book, Lesson 7

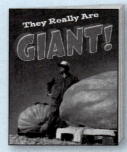

Trouble in the Lily Garden
Teacher's Edition, Lesson 7

They Really Are GIANT!
Student Book, Lesson 7

▶ The Ugly Vegetables

INTERACTIVE READ-ALOUD/SHARED READING

Read aloud the story to children. Stop periodically for very brief discussion of it. Use the following suggested stopping points and prompts for quick group response, or give a specific prompt and have partners or threes turn and talk.

- After the girl puts the vegetable labels in the ground, ask: "How is the girl's garden different from her neighbors' gardens?"
- After the vegetables begin to grow, ask: "What do you think will happen next in the garden? What makes you think so?"
- After the girl's mother makes the special soup, ask: "Do you agree with the girl's mother that her vegetables are better than flowers? Why or why not?"
- At the end of the story, ask: "What lesson did the girl learn in this story? Turn and talk about it with a partner."

MINILESSON Understanding Characters

TEACH Display the minilesson principle on chart paper, and read it aloud to children. Tell children they are going to learn to understand what characters are like from what they say and do.

1. Discuss the principle with children, using examples from *The Ugly Vegetables*. Suggested language: "In *The Ugly Vegetables*, the girl kept asking her mother why they were doing things differently in their garden than their neighbors were doing in theirs. What did this tell you about the girl?" *(She did not understand why her mother was not planting flowers. Perhaps she wanted their garden to be like all the other gardens in their neighborhood.)*

> **MINILESSON PRINCIPLE**
> Think about what characters say and do to help you learn about them.

2. Focus on the picture that shows the girl and her mother smelling the vegetable soup. Suggested language: "What was the girl's mother doing here? What did this tell you about her?" *(She was smelling the soup and looking pleased with it. She was probably very happy she grew the vegetables for this soup.)*

3. Focus children's attention on the page where the girl says *It was the best dinner ever*. Ask: "What do you think the neighbors were like? What did they do and say to make you think so?"

4. Use children's responses to the above questions to fill in a Column Chart like the one shown here. Help children understand how they can use this information to learn about each character.

Character	What Character Says	What Character Does

SUMMARIZE AND APPLY Restate the minilesson principle. Then tell children to apply it to their independent reading. Suggested language: "When you read, pay attention to what characters say and do. This will help you learn about them."

GROUP SHARE Ask children to describe a character they read about in independent reading. Have them tell what their character said and did and how that helped them learn about the character.

52 • Lesson 7

Lesson 7

▶ Trouble in the Lily Garden

INTERACTIVE READ-ALOUD/SHARED READING

Read aloud the story to children. Stop periodically for brief discussion. Use the following suggested stopping points and prompts:

- After Lia talks to Moe for the first time, ask: "Does this story seem more like real life or make-believe? What clues tell you so?"
- After Lia calls out to the lilies for the second time, ask: "What can you tell about Lia from what she says and does?"
- At the end, ask: "Was Lia right to be worried about the lilies? Turn and talk about your ideas with a partner."

MINILESSON Conclusions

TEACH Display the minilesson principle on chart paper, and read it aloud to children. Tell children they are going to learn how to use characters' words to understand what is happening in a story.

1. Focus children's attention on Lia's words in the story. Suggested language: "Why do you think Lia asked Moe about the slugs?" *(Possible answer: because he could see what was happening)*

> **MINILESSON PRINCIPLE**
>
> Think about what characters say to understand what is happening in the story.

2. Next, focus children's attention on Moe's words. Ask: "Why do you think Moe did not finish his sentence at the end of the story?" *(Possible answer: He was afraid to tell Lia what happened to her friends.)*

3. Help children use what they learned from the characters' words to draw a conclusion about why the north garden was silent when Lia called. Ask: "What do you think happened to the lilies in the north garden?" *(They were eaten by the slugs.)* Follow-up: "What clues did you get from Lia and Moe's words?" *(Lia said that slugs eat flowers; she said the north garden was quiet. Moe didn't finish his sentence when he looked at the north garden. The things they said made me think that the lilies in the north garden were in trouble.)*

SUMMARIZE AND APPLY Restate the minilesson principle. Tell children to apply it to their independent reading. Suggested language: "When you read, use characters' words to understand things that are happening in the story."

GROUP SHARE Have children tell how they used characters' words to understand stories they read for independent reading.

▶ They Really Are GIANT!

INTERACTIVE READ-ALOUD/SHARED READING

Read aloud the book to children. Stop periodically for brief discussion. Use the following suggested stopping points and prompts:

- After completing the section called World Record Breakers, ask: "What was amazing about the pumpkin that won Half Moon Bay's weigh-off in 2007?"
- After completing Home of the Giants, ask: "What was this book mostly about? How do you know? Share your ideas with a partner."

MINILESSON Genre: Informational Text

TEACH Write the minilesson principle on chart paper, and read it aloud to children. Explain to children that the author of *They Really Are GIANT!* used both words and pictures to give information about giant vegetables.

1. Remind children that some books include facts and information instead of telling a story. Have children identify some of the important facts and information from *They Really Are GIANT!* Suggested language: "What are some words the author used to tell what the vegetables were like?" *(biggest, super-sized, tender, delicious, giant, wrinkled)*

> **MINILESSON PRINCIPLE**
>
> Notice how the author tells what things are like.

2. Choose one of the vegetables mentioned in the book. Have children name words the author used to tell about that vegetable. Record children's responses in a Web. Guide children to notice how the author included facts about how big the vegetables could get, pictures of people with the giant vegetables, and even a chart showing how big they can get.

SUMMARIZE AND APPLY Restate the minilesson principle. Tell children to apply it to their independent reading. Suggested language: "As you read, pay attention to all the different ways the author lets you know what things are like."

GROUP SHARE Ask children to tell about other books they have read that included facts and information. Ask them to describe how the author of each book showed what things are like.

Whole-Group Lessons • 53

Whole-Group Lessons

Super Storms
Student Book, Lesson 8

Floods: Dangerous Water
Teacher's Edition, Lesson 8

Weather Poems
Student Book, Lesson 8

▶ Super Storms

INTERACTIVE READ-ALOUD/SHARED READING

Read aloud the book to children. Stop periodically for very brief discussion of it. Use the following suggested stopping points and prompts for quick group response, or give a specific prompt and have partners or threes turn and talk.

- After the paragraph about thunder, ask: "How can you tell how far away lightning is?"
- After the paragraph about tornado warnings, ask: "Why is it important to find shelter in a basement or closet during a tornado warning? Turn and talk about your ideas with a partner."
- After the paragraph about the eye of a hurricane, say: "Look at the photograph of the hurricane from above. Which part do you think is the eye? Why?"
- At the end, ask: "Why is it important to learn about different types of storms? Turn and talk about your ideas with a partner."

MINILESSON Main Idea and Details

TEACH Display the minilesson principle on chart paper, and read it aloud to children. Tell children they are going to learn how to think about the most important idea in a book as they read.

1. Discuss the principle with children, using examples of main ideas from *Super Storms*. Suggested language: "*Super Storms* is mostly about one idea. What is the book mostly about?" *(The book is mostly about different types of storms and what causes them.)* Follow-up: "In this book, each paragraph is also mostly about one idea. However, they all have one thing in common. They all tell about storms in some way."

MINILESSON PRINCIPLE
Notice what the text is mostly about.

2. Focus on one detail that supports the main idea, such as the details in the hailstone paragraph. Suggested language: "In the paragraph about hailstones, what did you learn?" *(Hailstones are chunks of ice that can be as small as a marble or bigger than a baseball. They sometimes come with thunderstorms and cause damage.)* Follow-up: "What was this paragraph mostly about?" *(what hailstones are like)*

3. Use children's responses to explain how details tell more information about the main idea of the book. Suggested language: "Each paragraph tells more about the main idea of the book. The information about hailstones tells us more about one type of storm."

4. Elicit from children additional details about storms from the book. Record children's ideas in a Web like the one shown here.

SUMMARIZE AND APPLY Restate the minilesson principle. Then tell children to apply it to their independent reading. Suggested language: "When you read, think about what the book is mostly about. Think about how the other information tells about that idea."

GROUP SHARE Ask children to talk about their book by telling what it is mostly about. Have them explain how information in the book tells about that idea.

54 • Lesson 8

Lesson 8

► Floods: Dangerous Water

INTERACTIVE READ-ALOUD/SHARED READING

Read aloud the selection to children. Stop periodically for brief discussion. Use the following suggested stopping points and prompts:

- After the first paragraph, ask: "How is water both important and dangerous to living things? Turn and talk about your ideas with a partner."
- After the third paragraph, say: "The author uses the words *like a sponge* in the first sentence of this paragraph. Why do you think the author didn't just say *the ground soaks up water*?"
- At the end of the selection, ask: "What might it be like to be in an area that flooded? Turn and talk about your ideas with a partner."

MINILESSON Main Idea and Details

TEACH Display the minilesson principle on chart paper, and read it aloud to children. Tell children that they are going to learn to think about what a book is mostly about.

1. Using *Floods: Dangerous Water,* remind children that a book is mostly about one main idea. Suggested language: "In *Floods: Dangerous Water,* you learned about how water is helpful but can also be very harmful. Was this book mostly about how water helps or how it harms?" *(harms)*

> **MINILESSON PRINCIPLE**
>
> Notice what the book is mostly about.

2. Talk with children about the ways in which water is harmful. Suggested language: "This book gives many details about how water can be harmful if there is too much. How can too much water be dangerous?" *(Too much water causes floods, which damage houses, cars, and people.)* Follow-up: "What can people do to prevent damage?" *(People can build levees or pile up bags of sand. People can also stay safe from floods by listening to warnings and staying in a safe area.)*

3. Write the main idea *Too much water can cause a dangerous flood* in the top box of an Idea-Support Map. Then have children give details that support what the book is mostly about. Record their ideas.

SUMMARIZE AND APPLY Restate the minilesson principle. Tell children to apply it to their independent reading. Suggested language: "When you read, think about what the book is mostly about to help you understand it."

GROUP SHARE Ask children to share a book from independent reading and tell what the book was mostly about.

► Weather Poems

INTERACTIVE READ-ALOUD/SHARED READING

Read aloud the introduction and poems to children. Stop periodically for brief discussion. Use the following suggested stopping points and prompts:

- After the first poem, ask: "What words are repeated in this poem?" Follow-up: "Why do you think the poet repeated certain words?"
- After the second poem, ask: "Why do you think the poet describes the umbrella as walking backward?"
- After the third poem, ask: "How does it make you feel to think about the Sun talking? Turn and talk about your answer with a partner."

MINILESSON Genre: Poetry

TEACH Remind children of ways that poems are different from other things they might read. Many poems rhyme or have repeated lines, for example. Poems also use words to help readers make pictures in their minds. Then write the minilesson principle on chart paper, and read it aloud for children.

1. Tell children to close their eyes. Then reread "Night Drumming for Rain" for children, having them listen for words that help them picture drumming for rain. Suggested language: "Which words help you picture someone drumming?" *(basket drum sounding)* Follow-up: "Which words help you picture the rain?" *(rumbling, humming)*

> **MINILESSON PRINCIPLE**
>
> Think about how words in a poem make pictures in your mind.

2. Repeat the first step using "Morning Sun." Have children name words that help them picture the Sun in the morning.

SUMMARIZE AND APPLY Restate the minilesson principle. Tell children to apply it to their independent reading. Suggested language: "When you read, think about how the author's words help you make pictures in your mind."

GROUP SHARE Ask children to tell about how they used words from their independent reading to make pictures in their minds.

Whole-Group Lessons • 55

Whole-Group Lessons

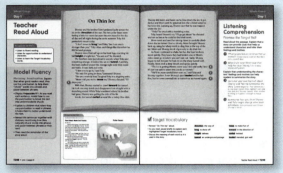

How Chipmunk Got His Stripes
Student Book, Lesson 9

On Thin Ice
Teacher's Edition, Lesson 9

Why Rabbits Have Short Tails
Student Book, Lesson 9

▶ How Chipmunk Got His Stripes

INTERACTIVE READ-ALOUD/SHARED READING

Read aloud the story to children. Stop periodically for very brief discussion of it. Use the following suggested stopping points and prompts for quick group response, or give a specific prompt and have partners or threes turn and talk.

- After Brown Squirrel challenges Bear to stop the sun from rising, ask: "What does Bear think of himself? How do you know that?"
- After the sun comes up, ask: "How do you think Bear and Brown Squirrel are feeling now? Turn and talk about your ideas with a partner."
- After Bear agrees that Brown Squirrel should apologize, ask: "What do you think Brown Squirrel is up to?" Follow-up: "What do you think will happen next?"
- At the end of the story, ask: "What lessons do Bear and Chipmunk learn?"

MINILESSON Understanding Characters

TEACH Display the minilesson principle on chart paper, and read it aloud to children. Tell children they are going to learn how to think about characters as they read.

1. Discuss the principle with children, using examples of characters from *How Chipmunk Got His Stripes*. Suggested language: "In the story *How Chipmunk Got His Stripes*, we got to know a few characters as we read. Who were these characters?" *(Brown Squirrel/Chipmunk, Bear)*

2. Focus on one character, such as Brown Squirrel. Suggested language: "In the middle of the story, Brown Squirrel thought his life was in danger, so he played a trick on Bear. What happened?" *(Brown Squirrel asked Bear to lift his paw so he could apologize for teasing Bear. When Bear lifted his paw, Brown Squirrel tried to get away.)*

3. Use children's responses to explain how what characters say and what they do are clues to what they are like. Suggested language: "The author used Brown Squirrel's words (what he said to Bear) and what he did (tried to get away) to show readers that Brown Squirrel was pretty clever."

4. Work with children to think about what Bear is like. Record children's ideas in a T-Map like the one shown here.

MINILESSON PRINCIPLE

Think about what characters say and do.

What Character Says and Does	What We Learn About the Character

SUMMARIZE AND APPLY Restate the minilesson principle. Then tell children to apply it to their independent reading. Suggested language: "When you read, think about what the characters say and do. Think about what you find out about the characters by what they say and do."

GROUP SHARE Ask children to share what they learned about one character in their story. Tell them to explain what the character said or did that helped them learn about the character.

56 • Lesson 9

Lesson 9

▶ On Thin Ice

INTERACTIVE READ-ALOUD/SHARED READING

Read aloud the story to children. Stop periodically for brief discussion of it. Use the following suggested stopping points and prompts:

- After Shoney raises himself up on his hind legs, ask: "What is happening with these two brothers?"
- After Shoney cries for help in the tunnel, ask: "Why does Shoney go in the tunnel? How is he probably feeling now?"
- At the end of the story, say: "Think about the whole story. What do you think the author is trying to tell you? Turn and talk about your ideas with a partner."

MINILESSON Understanding Characters

TEACH Display the minilesson principle on chart paper, and read it aloud to children. Tell children they are going to learn to think about what characters do and why.

1. Using the character Shoney from *On Thin Ice*, discuss with children that characters behave in certain ways for a reason. Suggested language: "In the story *On Thin Ice*, we read about Toby and Shoney, two polar bears who are brothers. Shoney did something in the story that was surprising. What was it?" *(Shoney crawled into a dark ice tunnel after his brother teased him.)*

> **MINILESSON PRINCIPLE**
>
> Think about what characters do and why.

2. Talk with children about Shoney's reason for crawling into the ice tunnel. Suggested language: "We learned in the story that Toby and Shoney argued about who was stronger and braver. Why did Shoney go into the ice tunnel?" *(to prove that he wasn't scared)*

3. Discuss with children reasons for characters' actions in other parts of the story. Write their ideas in a T-Map labeled *What the Character Does* and *Why*.

SUMMARIZE AND APPLY Restate the minilesson principle. Tell children to apply it to their independent reading. Suggested language: "When you read, think about what characters do and why to help you understand the story."

GROUP SHARE Ask children to share an example from independent reading of something a character did and why the character acted this way.

▶ Why Rabbits Have Short Tails

INTERACTIVE READ-ALOUD/SHARED READING

Read aloud the story to children. Stop periodically for brief discussion. Use the following suggested stopping points and prompts:

- After the author says that Rabbit does not like to be teased, ask: "What character have we learned about so far?" Follow-up: "What is Rabbit like?"
- At the end of the story, ask: "How did things turn out for Rabbit?" Follow-up: "How is Rabbit like some of the other characters we've read about this week? Turn and talk about your ideas with a partner."

MINILESSON Genre: Folktales

TEACH Remind children that they have read three stories this week: *How Chipmunk Got His Stripes, On Thin Ice,* and *Why Rabbits Have Short Tails.* Explain that the stories have something in common—they are a type of story called a folktale.

1. Focus on *Why Rabbits Have Short Tails* to introduce the idea that folktale characters often learn a lesson. Suggested language: "What kind of character was Rabbit?" *(He liked to brag and trick others.)* Follow-up: "Is it a good idea to brag and trick people?" *(no)* "Why not?" *(It is not nice to trick people because it makes other people angry.)*

> **MINILESSON PRINCIPLE**
>
> Notice that in folktales the characters learn an important lesson.

2. Guide children to understand what happened to Rabbit because he tried to trick Turtle. Suggested language: "What happened when Rabbit tried to trick Turtle?" *(Turtle got angry and snapped off Rabbit's tail. Rabbit learned that it is not a good idea to trick others.)*

3. Write the minilesson principle on chart paper, and discuss with children the lessons that the characters learned in *How Chipmunk Got His Stripes* and *On Thin Ice*. Explain to children that knowing to expect that a character will learn a lesson in a folktale will help them understand what they read.

SUMMARIZE AND APPLY Restate the minilesson principle. Tell children to apply it to their independent reading. Suggested language: "When you read a folktale, look for a lesson that a character learns."

GROUP SHARE Ask children to explain a lesson that a character learned in a story they read for independent reading.

Whole-Group Lessons • **57**

Whole-Group Lessons

Jellies
Student Book, Lesson 10

Sharks on the Run!
Teacher's Edition, Lesson 10

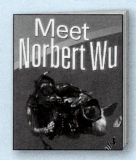

Meet Norbert Wu
Student Book, Lesson 10

▶ Jellies

INTERACTIVE READ-ALOUD/SHARED READING

Read aloud the book to children. Stop periodically for very brief discussion. Use the following suggested stopping points and prompts for quick group response, or give a specific prompt and have partners or threes turn and talk.

- After the paragraph about not worrying, ask: "Why can't jellyfish worry that other creatures are going to eat them?"
- After the paragraph about plastic trash, ask: "How are jellyfish and plastic trash the same? How are they different?"
- After the paragraph about the Arctic lion's mane jellyfish, say: "Look at the picture of the Arctic lion's mane jellyfish. Why do you think it has this name?"
- At the end of the book, ask: "Why does the author remind us that jellyfish don't have brains or hearts? Turn and talk about your ideas with a partner."

MINILESSON Fact and Opinion

TEACH Display the minilesson principle on chart paper, and read it aloud to children. Tell children they are going to learn how to notice the difference between words that can be proved and words that tell what an author thinks.

1. Discuss the principle with children, using example sentences from *Jellies*. Focus on the page with the moon jellyfish. Suggested language: "The author writes that jellyfish are almost all water and a little protein. Can these words be proved or are they what the author thinks? How do you know?" *(These words can be proved by looking in a science book or on the Internet to find out what jellyfish are made of.)*

   > **MINILESSON PRINCIPLE**
   > Notice that some of the author's words can be proved and some are what the author thinks.

2. Explain to children how to identify an opinion. Suggested language: "The author writes that jellyfish *look slimy and disgusting when they wash up on the beach.* Can these words be proved or are they what the author thinks? How do you know?" *(The word* disgusting *is a clue that this cannot be proved and is something the author thinks. Someone else might think jellyfish are pretty.)*

3. Use children's responses to explain that an author often uses both kinds of words in a book. Suggested language: "Some of the author's words can be proved by looking in a book or at a website. They are facts. Some of the author's words tell what the author thinks. They are the author's opinions."

4. Elicit from children additional examples of facts and opinions from the book. Record children's ideas in a T-Map like the one shown here.

What Can Be Proved	What the Author Thinks

SUMMARIZE AND APPLY Restate the minilesson principle. Then tell children to apply it to their independent reading. Suggested language: "When you read, think about the author's words. Think about which words can be proved and which words tell what the author thinks."

GROUP SHARE Ask children to share examples from their independent reading of words that can be proved and words that tell what the author thinks.

58 • Lesson 10

Lesson 10

▶ Sharks on the Run!

INTERACTIVE READ-ALOUD/SHARED READING

Read aloud the selection to children. Stop periodically for brief discussion. Use the following suggested stopping points and prompts:

- After the second paragraph, ask: "Why does the author explain that more people are killed each year by animals other than sharks?"
- After the fifth paragraph, ask: "Why do people kill sharks?"
- At the end, ask: "Why do you think the author wrote this book? Turn and talk about your ideas with a partner."

MINILESSON Fact and Opinion

TEACH Display the minilesson principle on chart paper, and read it aloud to children. Tell children they are going to learn to think about how the author uses words to show how he or she feels.

1. Using examples from *Sharks on the Run!*, discuss with children how the author feels. Suggested language: "In *Sharks on the Run!*, the author wrote about the problems facing sharks. How do you think the author feels about sharks?" *(The author is impressed by sharks and thinks they should be protected.)*

> **MINILESSON PRINCIPLE**
>
> Think about words the author uses to show how he feels.

2. Talk with children about what words the author uses to show how he feels. Suggested language: "An author's words can show how he feels. What words show that the author is impressed by sharks and thinks they should be protected?" *(The author says the sharks are amazing animals and that they do an important job in the ocean. The words* amazing *and* important *show that the author is impressed by sharks.)*

3. Reread the last three paragraphs of *Sharks on the Run!* and have children listen for words that show the author's feelings. Then have children name these words as you list them on chart paper. Tell children that they can use these words to understand how the author feels about sharks.

SUMMARIZE AND APPLY Restate the minilesson principle. Then tell children to apply it to their independent reading. Suggested language: "When you read, think about the words the author uses to show how he feels."

GROUP SHARE Ask children to share an example from independent reading of how an author feels and the words he or she used to show that feeling.

▶ Meet Norbert Wu

INTERACTIVE READ-ALOUD/SHARED READING

Read aloud the book to children. Stop periodically for brief discussion. Use the following suggested stopping points and prompts:

- After the first paragraph, ask: "Why does the author begin the story by telling us what Mr. Wu wears to his job?"
- After reading Choices to Make, Places to Go, ask: "Why do you think Mr. Wu has to travel for his job?"
- At the end, ask: "Would you like to have Norbert Wu's job? Turn and talk about your ideas with a partner."

MINILESSON Text and Graphic Features

TEACH Write the minilesson principle on chart paper. Explain to children that the author of *Meet Norbert Wu* used pictures and words to tell them more about the topic.

1. Point out to children that the author of *Meet Norbert Wu* used certain types of words and pictures. Suggested language: "In *Meet Norbert Wu*, the author included a picture of Mr. Wu in his special underwater gear. The author wrote labels for this picture to tell more about it. These pictures and words help us understand what Norbert Wu's job is like."

> **MINILESSON PRINCIPLE**
>
> Think about how pictures and words tell more about the topic.

2. Read the labels with children and talk about what they've learned from the picture and labels. Suggested language: "What are the important parts of Mr. Wu's underwater gear?" *(camera, air tank, and flippers)* "How does the author help you learn about these parts?" *(The author tells about each part and uses arrows to point to each part in the picture.)*

3. Help children understand that authors include pictures and words to tell more about the topic. Explain to children that paying attention to the pictures and the words that tell about them will help them understand the topic better.

SUMMARIZE AND APPLY Restate the minilesson principle. Tell children to apply it to their independent reading. Suggested language: "When you read, think about how pictures and words tell more about the topic."

GROUP SHARE Ask children to tell how pictures and words helped them learn more about the topic from their independent reading.

Whole-Group Lessons • **59**

Whole-Group Lessons

Click, Clack, Moo: Cows That Type
Student Book, Lesson 11

Don't Play Cards with a Dog in the Room!
Teacher's Edition, Lesson 11

Talk About Smart Animals!
Student Book, Lesson 11

▶ Click, Clack, Moo: Cows That Type

INTERACTIVE READ-ALOUD/SHARED READING

Read aloud the story to children. Stop periodically for very brief discussion of it. Use the following suggested stopping points and prompts for quick group response, or give a specific prompt and have partners or threes turn and talk.

- After the second refrain of *clickety, clack, moo*, ask: "What do you think the cows are typing?"
- After the cows post the *No milk today* note, ask: "What do you think a *strike* is?"
- After the cows and hens get their blankets, ask: "Do you think Farmer Brown made a good deal?" Follow-up: "What do you think will happen next?"
- At the end, ask: "Why do you think the author wrote this story? Turn and talk about your ideas with a partner."

MINILESSON Conclusions

TEACH Display the minilesson principle on chart paper, and read it aloud to children. Tell children they are going to learn how to notice clues about characters as they read. Explain to children that the clues will help them figure out how a character feels.

1. Discuss the principle with children, using examples of characters from *Click, Clack, Moo*. Suggested language: "In *Click, Clack, Moo*, you read about a farmer and some of his unusual animals. What made the farm animals in this story so unusual?" (*They typed notes to the farmer.*) Follow-up: "What kinds of notes did they type?" (*They typed notes asking for things and notes that said they were on strike.*)

2. Focus on the character Farmer Brown. Suggested language: "Farmer Brown got a note from the cows saying they won't give milk. What did he do when he saw the note?" (*He raised his fists over his head. He cried* No milk!)

3. Use children's responses to explain how authors give clues about how characters feel. Suggested language: "What Farmer Brown did and said gave clues about how he felt. You can see from the picture that he was raising his fists. You read that he cried *No milk!* Both of these clues tell you that Farmer Brown was upset and angry."

4. Work with children to draw conclusions about other characters' feelings in the story. Record children's ideas in an Inference Map like the one shown here.

> **MINILESSON PRINCIPLE**
> Think about clues in the story that show how characters feel.

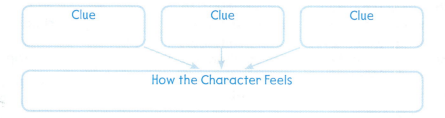

SUMMARIZE AND APPLY Restate the minilesson principle. Then tell children to apply it to their independent reading. Suggested language: "When you read a story, look for clues that help you figure out how a character feels."

GROUP SHARE Have children tell about the feelings of a character in a book they are reading. Ask them to share clues from the book that support their ideas about the character's feelings.

Lesson 11

▶ Don't Play Cards with a Dog in the Room!

INTERACTIVE READ-ALOUD/SHARED READING

Read aloud the story to children. Stop periodically for brief discussion of it. Use the following suggested stopping points and prompts:

- After the first page, ask: "What is a superstition?"
- After the grandmother's advice, ask: "Would you take the grandmother's advice? Why or why not?"
- At the end of the story, ask: "What superstitions do you know? Turn and talk with a partner about different superstitions."

MINILESSON Conclusions

TEACH Display the minilesson principle on chart paper, and read it aloud to children. Tell children they are going to think about how authors give clues to how they feel about a topic.

1. Discuss the principle with children, using *Don't Play Cards with a Dog in the Room!* as an example. Focus on one superstition from the story, such as *Step on a crack, break your mother's back.* Suggested language: "The author gives clues about her feelings about superstitions. Right before the mention of *Step on a crack, break your mother's back*, what words does the author use to describe superstitions?" (*problem, impossible*)

> **MINILESSON PRINCIPLE**
>
> Think about clues the author gives to figure out how he or she feels about the topic.

2. Use children's responses to explain that authors often give clues about how they feel about a topic. Suggested language: "You can tell that the author wants you to realize that this superstition is silly. The author points out how this superstition could not possibly be true. Knowing the author's feelings helps you better understand the writing."

3. Help children identify other clues from the story that help them figure out how the author feels. Write their ideas in an Inference Map labeled *Clue, Clue, Clue,* and *Author's Feelings.*

SUMMARIZE AND APPLY Restate the minilesson principle. Tell children to apply it to their independent reading. Suggested language: "When you read, look for clues that tell you how the author feels about the topic."

GROUP SHARE Have children share how they think the author feels about the topic of their book for independent reading. Ask them to share clues from the book that show how the author feels.

▶ Talk About Smart Animals!

INTERACTIVE READ-ALOUD/SHARED READING

Read aloud the book to children. Stop periodically for brief discussion of it. Use the following suggested stopping points and prompts:

- After the second page, ask: "How does the picture help you understand what Rio does?"
- After reading about Alex, ask: "Which of Alex's skills do you think is most amazing? Why?"
- At the end, ask: "How are Rio and Alex the same, and how are they different? Turn and talk about your ideas with a partner."

MINILESSON Text and Graphic Features

TEACH Explain to children that *Talk About Smart Animals!* is an informational book. It gives information about two real animals.

1. Focus on the headings to introduce how authors call attention to and organize information. Suggested language: "In *Talk About Smart Animals!,* the author included some words in red type. These words are also darker than the words that follow them."

> **MINILESSON PRINCIPLE**
>
> Notice headings to think about what each section is about.

2. Page through the text with children to identify the two headings in red, bold type. Point out how each heading tells what the paragraph is going to be about. Suggested language: "Look at the words *This Sea Lion Can Match*. They are in a different color and bigger than the words that follow them. If you read the section, you can see that the sentences all tell about a sea lion who can match pictures. If you want to find information about a sea lion who matches, you can easily find it by looking for the heading that names the section."

3. Write the minilesson principle on chart paper, and read it aloud to children. Guide them to see how the headings stand out from the other words. Explain to children that authors use headings to help readers understand what each section is about.

SUMMARIZE AND APPLY Restate the minilesson principle. Explain to children that they can apply it to their independent reading. Suggested language: "When you read, look for headings that tell what sections are about."

GROUP SHARE Ask children to share examples of headings in a book they read. Have them tell how the headings helped them understand the information in each section.

Whole-Group Lessons • 61

Whole-Group Lessons

Violet's Music
Student Book, Lesson 12

Rita Breaks the Rules
Teacher's Edition, Lesson 12

Wolfgang Mozart, Child Superstar
Student Book, Lesson 12

▶ Violet's Music

INTERACTIVE READ-ALOUD/SHARED READING

Read aloud the story to children. Stop periodically for very brief discussion of it. Use the following suggested stopping points and prompts for quick group response, or give a specific prompt and have partners or threes turn and talk.

- After reading about Violet in her nursery, ask: "What makes Violet different from most babies?" Follow-up: "How do you think she will feel about music as she gets older?"
- After the pages that tell about kindergarten, ask: "How do you think Violet feels when she discovers no one else in her class wants to play music all day long?"
- After Violet plays a real guitar on a park bench, ask: "What makes this page different from the pages that have come before it? Turn and talk with your partner about what you think will happen next."
- At the end of the story, ask: "What words and phrases were repeated in the story?" Follow-up: "How did the repeated words and phrases help you enjoy the story?"

MINILESSON Story Structure

TEACH Display the minilesson principle on chart paper, and read it aloud to children. Tell children they are going to learn how to think about the problem in a story.

1. Discuss the principle with children, using examples from *Violet's Music*. Suggested language: "Who was the main character in this story?" (*Violet*) Follow-up: "What made her special?" (*She wanted to play music all day long.*) "What was she trying to find?" (*other children who were just like her*)

    > **MINILESSON PRINCIPLE**
    > Think about the problem in the story.

2. Use children's responses to highlight the story's problem. Suggested language: "In the story *Violet's Music*, you learned about a problem at the beginning of the story. What problem did Violet have?" (*She could not find other children who wanted to play music all day long.*)

3. Record children's ideas in a Story Map like the one shown here. List the problem under *Beginning*. Then work with students to complete the Story Map by telling what happens with Violet's problem in the middle of the story and at the end.

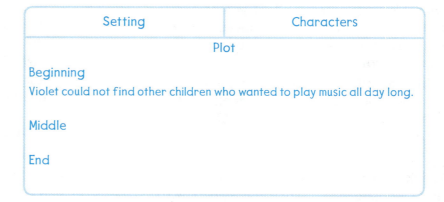

SUMMARIZE AND APPLY Restate the minilesson principle. Then tell children to apply it to their independent reading. Suggested language: "When you read a story, think about the problem the character has."

GROUP SHARE Have children share the problem in the story they read during independent reading.

Lesson 12

▶ Rita Breaks the Rules

INTERACTIVE READ-ALOUD/SHARED READING

Read aloud the story to children. Stop periodically for brief discussion of it. Use the following suggested stopping points and prompts:

- After the first paragraph, ask: "How would you describe Miguel?"
- After the first page, ask: "What do you think Miguel is going to do next?"
- At the end of the story, ask: "Do you think Miguel is a good older brother? Turn and talk with a partner about your ideas."

MINILESSON Story Structure

TEACH Display the minilesson principle on chart paper, and read it aloud to children. Tell children they are going to think about where a story takes place in order to help them picture what happens in the story.

1. Focus on the setting of *Rita Breaks the Rules* to help children picture what happens. Suggested language: "In the story *Rita Breaks the Rules*, most of the story took place in Miguel's bedroom. Thinking about how the place changed can help you understand what happened in a story."

> **MINILESSON PRINCIPLE**
>
> Think about where the story takes place to help you picture what happens.

2. Draw two Webs and label one *Before* and one *After*. In the center ovals of each Web, write *Miguel's Room*. Have children give details about the room before and after Rita made a mess, and record their ideas in the outer ovals. Suggested language: "What details did you learn about Miguel's bedroom before and after Rita made a mess?"

3. Use children's responses to point out how this description of the setting helps readers picture what happens. Suggested language: "When Miguel found his baby sister in the middle of a mess, knowing what his room once looked like helps you imagine how upsetting it must have been to Miguel. When Miguel was nice to his sister, it also helps you realize how much he loves his sister because he didn't get mad at her."

SUMMARIZE AND APPLY Restate the minilesson principle. Tell children to apply it to their independent reading. Suggested language: "When you read a story, think about where it takes place. Make a picture in your mind to help you understand what is happening."

GROUP SHARE Ask children to describe the setting of a story they are reading or have read. Ask them to share how picturing where the story took place helped them understand what happened.

▶ Wolfgang Mozart, Child Superstar

INTERACTIVE READ-ALOUD/SHARED READING

Read aloud the biography to children. Stop periodically for brief discussion of it. Use the following suggested stopping points and prompts:

- After the second page, ask: "How does the timeline help you better understand the information?"
- At the end, ask: "Why do you think the title of this piece of writing includes the words *Child Superstar*? Turn and talk about your ideas with a partner."

MINILESSON Genre: Biography

TEACH Explain to children that *Wolfgang Mozart, Child Superstar* is different from the other two stories they read this week. Point out to children that it is a biography. It gives information and facts about the life of a real person.

1. Introduce the idea that an author writing a biography tells what is special about the person. Suggested language: "In *Wolfgang Mozart, Child Superstar*, the author gave details about Mozart's young life in both the words and the timeline. All the details told about the special things Mozart did. What were some of those special things?" (*He learned how to play the harpsichord at three. By five, he wrote his own music. He played music all over Europe with his family.*)

> **MINILESSON PRINCIPLE**
>
> Notice how the author tells what is special about the person he is writing about.

2. Guide children to tell why these things were special. Suggested language: "What is special about learning to play the harpsichord at age three?" (*Most children don't learn to play instruments until they are much older; he was very special to learn this at such a young age.*)

3. Guide children to tell why other events in Mozart's life were special as you write the minilesson principle on chart paper. Explain to children that when they read a biography, thinking about why the person's life was special will help them understand what they read.

SUMMARIZE AND APPLY Restate the minilesson principle. Tell children to apply it to their independent reading. Suggested language: "When you read, think about what is special about the person you are reading about."

GROUP SHARE Ask children to explain what is special about the person they read about for independent reading.

Whole-Group Lessons • **63**

Whole-Group Lessons

Schools Around the World
Student Book, Lesson 13

One-Room Schoolhouse
Teacher's Edition, Lesson 13

School Poems
Student Book, Lesson 13

▶ **Schools Around the World**

INTERACTIVE READ-ALOUD/SHARED READING

Read aloud the book to children. Stop periodically for very brief discussion of it. Use the following suggested stopping points and prompts for quick group response, or give a specific prompt and have partners or threes turn and talk.

- After the Other Lessons section, ask: "How do the pictures and captions help you better understand the information on this page?"
- After the School Chores section, ask: "What chores do you have to do at school?" Follow-up: "How are they the same as chores in this book?"
- At the end of the book, ask: "Why do you think people all around the world have some kind of school? Turn and talk to a partner about the reasons for having schools."

MINILESSON Author's Purpose

TEACH Display the minilesson principle on chart paper, and read it aloud to children. Tell children they are going to learn to think about why the author wrote a book and what they should learn by reading it.

1. Discuss the principle with children, using examples from *Schools Around the World*. Suggested language: "In *Schools Around the World*, each section gave information. What did all of the sections tell about?" (*schools*) Follow-up: "What were some of the different sections about?" (*what schools look like, what students do in school, different kinds of schools*)

2. Focus on the section The School Day. Suggested language: "What did the author tell about the school day?" (*The author told what students do during the day. The author told how school days can be the same or different.*) Follow-up: "What do you think the author wanted you to learn?" (*The author wanted me to learn that all schools around the world have teachers and students. She also wanted me to learn about different things students do during the school day, such as work in groups or go on field trips.*)

3. Use children's responses to explain that authors write for a reason. Suggested language: "An author can write for different reasons. In this book, the author gives a lot of information. This gives you a clue that the author wrote to teach you about a topic."

4. Work with children to identify other clues that support the idea that the author wrote the book to teach about a topic. Record children's ideas in an Inference Map.

> **MINILESSON PRINCIPLE**
> Think about why the author wrote the book and what you should learn.

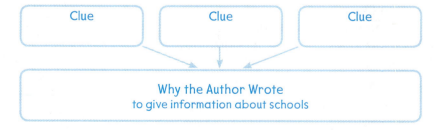

SUMMARIZE AND APPLY Restate the minilesson principle. Then tell children to apply it to their independent reading. Suggested language: "When you read, think about why the author wrote the book and what you should learn from it."

GROUP SHARE Have children tell why an author wrote a book they read for independent reading. Then have them tell what they learned.

64 • Lesson 13

Lesson 13

▶ One-Room Schoolhouse

INTERACTIVE READ-ALOUD/SHARED READING

Read aloud the selection to children. Stop periodically for brief discussion of it. Use the following suggested stopping points and prompts:

- After the second paragraph, ask: "How do you get to school? Tell how it is the same as or different from the way mentioned in *One-Room Schoolhouse*."
- After the first page, ask: "Would you enjoy being in a classroom with students from all grades? Turn and talk with a partner about how having students of different ages might be both good and bad."
- At the end, ask: "How has school changed in the past hundred years?" Follow-up: "What part of school from long ago do you wish you could experience today?"

MINILESSON Genre: Informational Text

TEACH Display the minilesson principle on chart paper, and read it aloud to children. Tell children they are going to think about how the author showed what going to a one-room schoolhouse was like.

1. Tell children that authors often use words that help readers picture what something is like. Suggested language: "In *One-Room Schoolhouse*, the author used words that help you understand what it looked and felt like to be in a one-room school. Do you remember what the author said you would see in the classroom?" (*hooks for coats, shelves for tin lunch pails, a long bench to sit on, slate chalkboards, a wood stove*)

> **MINILESSON PRINCIPLE**
>
> Notice how the author shows what things are like.

2. Work with children to name other descriptive details from the selection. Write their ideas in a Web with *One-Room Schoolhouse* in the center circle. Have children suggest details that tell what a one-room school was like. Write their ideas in the outer circles.

SUMMARIZE AND APPLY Restate the minilesson principle. Explain to children that they should apply it to their independent reading. Suggested language: "When you read, notice how the author shows what things are like."

GROUP SHARE Have children choose a description they have read in a book. Ask them to share words the author used to tell what something is like. You may wish to have the group tell which words helped them best picture the thing being described.

▶ School Poems

INTERACTIVE READ-ALOUD/SHARED READING

Read aloud the introduction and poems to children. Stop periodically for brief discussion of the poems. Use the following suggested stopping points and prompts:

- After the poem "School," ask: "What is being described in the first three lines?" Follow-up: "What do you think the poet means? Turn and talk about your ideas with a partner."
- After the poem "The Best," ask: "What do you think the poet means when she says *It's like listening to a hug*?"

MINILESSON Genre: Poetry

TEACH Remind children that they have read three poems: "School," "The Best," and "I Have to Write a Poem for Class." Display the minilesson principle on chart paper. Explain that some poems have words that rhyme, or have the same ending sounds. Rhyming words can make poems fun to read.

1. Model how to notice rhyming words in poems. Read aloud the first four lines of "I Have to Write a Poem for Class," emphasizing the rhyming words. Have children follow along. Suggested language: "Notice the sound of the words *succeed* and *need*. These words rhyme because they have the same ending sound."

> **MINILESSON PRINCIPLE**
>
> Notice that some poems have words that rhyme.

2. Read aloud the remaining lines of "I Have to Write a Poem for Class," and help children identify the rhyming words *be/poetry*, *rhyme/time*, and *good/should*.

3. For the other two poems, reread pairs of lines or stanzas at a time. Then ask children to name the words that rhyme.

SUMMARIZE AND APPLY Restate the minilesson principle. Tell children to apply it to their independent reading. Suggested language: "When you read poems, notice that some of them have words that rhyme."

GROUP SHARE Ask children to describe poems they read for independent reading. Have them tell whether the poems contained rhyming words.

Whole-Group Lessons • **65**

Whole-Group Lessons

Helen Keller
Student Book, Lesson 14

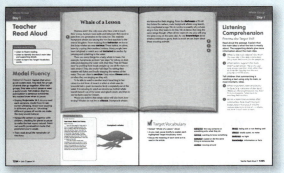

Whale of a Lesson
Teacher's Edition, Lesson 14

Talking Tools
Student Book, Lesson 14

▶ Helen Keller

INTERACTIVE READ-ALOUD/SHARED READING

Read aloud the book to children. Stop periodically for very brief discussion of it. Use the following suggested stopping points and prompts for quick group response, or give a specific prompt and have partners or threes turn and talk.

- After reading about Helen's motions, ask: "Why did Helen make these motions?"
- After reading about Helen's anger, ask: "How do you think Helen felt being alone in silence and darkness? Turn and talk with a partner about what it would be like to be blind and deaf."
- After reading that Helen did not know the names of things she touched, ask: "How did Annie teach Helen words?"
- At the end of the book, ask: "What can you learn from reading about Helen Keller? Turn and talk about your ideas with a partner."

MINILESSON Main Idea and Details

TEACH Display the minilesson principle on chart paper, and read it aloud to children. Tell children they are going to learn how to think about the most important things that happened in Helen Keller's life.

1. Discuss the principle with children, using the main idea from *Helen Keller*. Suggested language: "*Helen Keller* is a biography, which means it is mostly about the life of one person. What part of Helen's life is the book mostly about?" (*The book is mostly about her childhood and how she learned to communicate.*)

   > **MINILESSON PRINCIPLE**
   > Think about the most important things that happened in a person's life.

2. Focus on one detail that supports the main idea, such as the details in the section when Annie came to teach Helen. Suggested language: "In one section of the book, the author tells us how Annie taught Helen to communicate. What did you learn about how Helen learned to communicate?" (*Annie taught Helen to spell words with her fingers.*)

3. Use children's responses to explain that these details tell about the most important things that happened in a person's life. Suggested language: "Helen's life changed after she learned to communicate. This event was an important part of her life."

4. Elicit from children additional details about Helen Keller's childhood. Record children's ideas in an Idea-Support Map like the one shown here.

SUMMARIZE AND APPLY Restate the minilesson principle. Then tell children to apply it to their independent reading. Suggested language: "When you read a biography, think about the most important things that happened to the person you are reading about."

GROUP SHARE Ask children to talk about a book from their independent reading by telling what it is mostly about. Then have them explain the most important things that happened to a person in the book.

Lesson 14

▶ Whale of a Lesson

INTERACTIVE READ-ALOUD/SHARED READING

Read aloud the selection to children. Stop periodically for brief discussion. Use the following suggested stopping points and prompts:

- After the first paragraph, ask: "What does the word *imitated* mean?" Follow-up: "Why do calves copy their mother's actions?"
- After the third paragraph, ask: "How do mother whales teach their babies to breach?"
- At the end, ask: "Why do you think we do not know exactly why whales sing songs?"

MINILESSON Main Idea and Details

TEACH Display the minilesson principle on chart paper, and read it aloud to children. Tell children that they are going to learn to think about what a book is mostly about.

1. Using *Whale of a Lesson*, discuss with children that a book is about one main idea. Suggested language: "In *Whale of a Lesson*, you learned about whales. What is it mostly about?" (*It is mostly about how baby whales learn how to do things by copying their mothers.*)

> **MINILESSON PRINCIPLE**
>
> Notice that the author tells mostly about one idea and gives information about the idea.

2. Talk with children about the details that give information about the most important idea. Suggested language: "The author gives information about whales learning from their mothers. What are some of the things they learn?" (*Calves learn how to make certain motions, like pec slaps, head rises, and tail slaps. They also learn how to breach and sing.*)

3. Discuss with children that the author tells mostly about one idea and gives information about that idea. Write their ideas in an Idea-Support Map labeled *What Whales Learn*.

SUMMARIZE AND APPLY Restate the minilesson principle. Tell children to apply it to their independent reading. Suggested language: "When you read, notice how the author tells mostly about one idea. Pay attention to the information about that idea."

GROUP SHARE Ask children to explain what a book they read is mostly about. Then have them explain the information the author gives about that idea.

▶ Talking Tools

INTERACTIVE READ-ALOUD/SHARED READING

Read aloud the book to children. Stop periodically for brief discussion of the text. Use the following suggested stopping points and prompts:

- After the first page, ask: "How does a talking ATM help a blind person?"
- At the end of the book, ask: "How are Braille and Helen Keller's ways of communicating the same? How are they different?"

MINILESSON Text and Graphic Features

TEACH Write the minilesson principle on chart paper. Explain to children that they will learn to notice how words and pictures go together.

1. Point out to children that the author of *Talking Tools* used certain words and pictures to tell information. Suggested language: "In *Talking Tools,* the author included a photograph of a Braille notetaker. The author wrote labels and a caption for this picture to show how the notetaker works."

> **MINILESSON PRINCIPLE**
>
> Notice how words and pictures go together to explain ideas.

2. Guide children to look at the picture of the phone and discuss the information in the labels and caption. Suggested language: "What does the picture show?" (*a phone*) Follow-up: "How do the words and pictures go together to tell about the phone?" (*The picture shows what the phone looks like. The words explain the different parts that help blind people use the phone.*)

3. Guide children to talk about what they've learned from the picture, labels, and captions. Help children understand that authors include both pictures and words to explain ideas. Explain to children that paying attention to how words and pictures go together will help them understand ideas better.

SUMMARIZE AND APPLY Restate the minilesson principle. Tell children to apply it to their independent reading. Suggested language: "When you read, notice how words and pictures go together to explain ideas."

GROUP SHARE Ask children to tell how words and pictures helped them to understand ideas from their independent reading.

Whole-Group Lessons • **67**

Whole-Group Lessons

Officer Buckle and Gloria
Student Book, Lesson 15

Adventures at Scout Camp
Teacher's Edition, Lesson 15

Safety at Home
Student Book, Lesson 15

▶ **Officer Buckle and Gloria**

INTERACTIVE READ-ALOUD/SHARED READING

Read aloud the story to children. Stop periodically for very brief discussion of it. Use the following suggested stopping points and prompts for quick group response, or give a specific prompt and have partners or threes turn and talk.

- After Officer Buckle tells Mrs. Toppel never to stand on a swivel chair, say: "Look at the pictures. How do you think Officer Buckle thought up Safety Tip #77?"
- After Officer Buckle's first safety speech, ask: "Why were the kids clapping and cheering during Officer Buckle's safety speech?"
- At the end of the story, ask: "What did Officer Buckle learn from his own safety speeches? Turn and talk about your ideas with a partner."

MINILESSON Cause and Effect

TEACH Display the minilesson principle on chart paper, and read it aloud to children. Tell children they are going to learn to think about how one thing in a story makes another thing happen.

1. Discuss the principle with children, using examples from *Officer Buckle and Gloria*. Suggested language: "In the story *Officer Buckle and Gloria*, Gloria acted out Officer Buckle's safety tips during his speeches. What happened when she did that?" *(All the kids in the audience paid attention. Then, they laughed and clapped.)*

2. Focus on the event to help children see how the first event causes the second event to happen. Suggested language: "What happens when you see something funny?" *(You laugh or smile. You keep watching the funny thing to see if it will be funny again.)* Follow-up: "What happened because Gloria was funny?" *(The students watched Gloria and listened to Officer Buckle.)*

3. Tell children that when they read, they should think about what happens in a story and why. Suggested language: "What happened when other schools heard about Officer Buckle's safety speech with Gloria?" *(Other schools invited him to give safety speeches at their schools. He went to 313 schools.)* Follow-up: "What happened after Officer Buckle realized no one was watching him during the speeches?" *(He quit giving speeches and sent Gloria alone to stand on stage.)*

4. Help children identify other events in the story that happened because of a previous event. Record their ideas in a T-Map like the one shown here.

> **MINILESSON PRINCIPLE**
>
> Notice when one thing in a story makes another thing happen.

What Happened	What Made It Happen

SUMMARIZE AND APPLY Restate the minilesson principle. Then tell children to apply it to their independent reading. Suggested language: "When you read a story, think about what happens in the story. Look for things that make other things happen."

GROUP SHARE Have children choose a story event from their independent reading to share. Have them tell how this thing made another thing in the story happen.

Lesson 15

▶ Adventures at Scout Camp

INTERACTIVE READ-ALOUD/SHARED READING

Read aloud the story to children. Stop periodically for brief discussion. Use the following suggested stopping points and prompts:

- After the first paragraph, ask: "Why do you think is it important to always have a buddy at scout camp?"
- After the second paragraph, ask: "How does Quincy communicate with the other campers?" Follow-up: "How do the other campers learn from Quincy?"
- At the end of the story, ask: "How did all the signing practice help Jack and Quincy when Jack broke his leg?" Follow-up: "Why is communication with a buddy important?"

MINILESSON Cause and Effect

TEACH Display the minilesson principle on chart paper, and read it aloud to children. Tell children they are going to learn how one thing in a story makes another thing happen.

1. Remind children that events in a story make other events happen. Suggested language: "In the story *Adventures at Scout Camp*, what made the campers learn how to sign?" (*Their fellow camper, Quincy, was deaf.*)

> **MINILESSON PRINCIPLE**
>
> Notice when one thing in a story makes another thing happen.

2. Point out to children that many events are connected because one event can make another event happen. Suggested language: "Jack broke his leg. What made this happen?" (*He climbed onto a rock shelf to rest while hiking. The rock broke free, and he fell.*)
3. Work with children to discuss how events in the story made other events happen. Record children's ideas in a T-Map. Help children to understand that a story can be made up of a series of events that make other events happen.

SUMMARIZE AND APPLY Restate the minilesson principle. Tell children to apply it to their independent reading. Suggested language: "When you read, notice how one thing in a story makes another thing happen."

GROUP SHARE Have children choose a story event from their independent reading to share. Have them tell how this thing made another thing in the story happen.

▶ Safety at Home

INTERACTIVE READ-ALOUD/SHARED READING

Read aloud the play to children. Stop periodically for brief discussion. Use the following suggested stopping points and prompts:

- After Jake says *Look at our poster*, ask: "What information do you learn by reading the poster?"
- At the end of the play, ask: "Why do you think the author wrote this play?"

MINILESSON Genre: Play

TEACH Display the minilesson principle on chart paper, and read it aloud. Explain to children that the author wrote *Safety at Home* as a play. Have them tell how the play looks different from other stories they have read.

1. Talk about the format of a play with children. Suggested language: "A play has a title. It also has a cast, or a list of the characters in the play. Who is in the cast of this play?" (*Dad, Alexa, Jake*)

> **MINILESSON PRINCIPLE**
>
> Readers notice the parts of a play.

2. Page through the play with children to note other parts of a play. Point out that the words that come after the characters' names are the words that the characters say. Suggested language: "The characters' words tell the story. They tell what the characters do and how they feel. Read the words as the characters would say them. This will help you understand how the characters feel."

SUMMARIZE AND APPLY Restate the minilesson principle. Tell children to apply it to their independent reading. Suggested language: "When you read a play, pay attention to the different parts of the play."

GROUP SHARE Ask children to read aloud examples of dialogue in a play they have read. Then have children point out the different parts of the play.

Whole-Group Lessons • **69**

Whole-Group Lessons

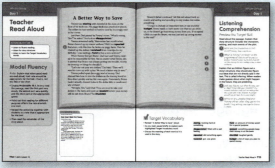

Mr. Tanen's Tie Trouble
Student Book, Lesson 16

A Better Way to Save
Teacher's Edition, Lesson 16

Playground Fun!
Student Book, Lesson 16

▶ Mr. Tanen's Tie Trouble

INTERACTIVE READ-ALOUD/SHARED READING

Read aloud the story to children. Stop periodically for very brief discussion of it. Use the following suggested stopping points and prompts for quick group response, or give a specific prompt and have partners or threes turn and talk.

- After Kaylee and Alex bring the money jar to Mr. Tanen, ask: "Who are Kaylee and Alex? What do they do?"
- After Mr. Apple buys the Crabapple tie, say: "Look at the names and pictures of Mr. Tanen's ties. Why do you think the ties are so important to Mr. Tanen?"
- After the auction, say: "Mr. Tanen tells the audience, *The more you give, the more you get*. What does that mean? Turn and talk with your partner about what Mr. Tanen is trying to say."
- At the end of the story, ask: "How do you think Mr. Tanen feels at the end of the story? Why?" Follow-up: "When has someone done something nice for you or when have you done something nice for someone else? How did it make you feel?"

MINILESSON Story Structure

TEACH Display the minilesson principle on chart paper, and read it aloud to children. Tell children they are going to think about the problem in a story and how it is solved.

1. Discuss the principle with children, using the main problem from *Mr. Tanen's Tie Trouble*. Suggested language: "In *Mr. Tanen's Tie Trouble*, you learned about a problem at the beginning of the story. What was the problem?" *(The playground was falling apart. There was not enough money to fix it.)*

2. Focus on how Mr. Tanen raised money to fix the playground. Suggested language: "How did Mr. Tanen solve the problem with the playground?" *(He sold his ties in an auction to raise money.)*

3. Explain to children that many stories have a problem that needs to be solved. Suggested language: "Most stories have a problem, or something that must be worked out. The events in the story tell how the problem is solved. In *Mr. Tanen's Tie Trouble*, there was no money to fix the playground. Mr. Tanen solved the problem by selling his ties."

4. Work with children to think about other problems in the story, such as the fact that Mr. Tanen missed his ties after he sold them, and how these problems are solved. Record children's ideas in a Story Map like the one shown here.

> **MINILESSON PRINCIPLE**
> Think about the problem in the story and how it is solved.

SUMMARIZE AND APPLY Restate the minilesson principle. Explain to children that they can apply it to their independent reading. Suggested language: "When you read a story, think about the problem in the story and how it is solved."

GROUP SHARE Have children share a problem in a story from their independent reading. Then ask them to tell how it was solved.

70 • Lesson 16

Lesson 16

▶ A Better Way to Save

INTERACTIVE READ-ALOUD/SHARED READING

Read aloud the story to children. Stop periodically for brief discussion. Use the following suggested stopping points and prompts:

- After Timmy explains what happened to his money, ask: "Why was the money important to Timmy?"
- After Timmy and his Dad clean up the money, ask: "What steps do Timmy and his Dad take to rescue the money?"
- At the end of the story, say: "At the end of the story, Timmy's dad said that spending money can save money. Turn and talk with a partner about what he meant."

MINILESSON Story Structure

TEACH Display the minilesson principle on chart paper, and read it aloud to children. Tell children they are going to notice how the problem in a story is solved.

1. Remind children that a story can have a problem that has to be solved. Suggested language: "In *A Better Way to Save,* Timmy had a problem right at the beginning of the story. What was the problem?" *(Bruno, the dog, has chewed Timmy's money.)*

> **MINILESSON PRINCIPLE**
>
> Notice how the problem in the story is solved.

2. Point out to children that they can pay attention to story events to figure out how the problem is solved. Suggested language: "Let's look at how Timmy and his dad solve the problem in the story. They dry out the money and decide to put it in a bank to keep it safe."

3. Work with children to retell the story and summarize how the problem in the story was solved. Write the ideas in a Story Map labeled *Problem, Events,* and *Solution.*

SUMMARIZE AND APPLY Restate the minilesson principle. Explain to children that they should apply it to their independent reading. Suggested language: "When you read, notice how the problem in a story is solved."

GROUP SHARE Have children choose a problem in a story they read and explain what it is. Then have them tell how the problem is solved in the story.

▶ Playground Fun!

INTERACTIVE READ-ALOUD/SHARED READING

Read aloud the book to children. Stop periodically for brief discussion. Use the following suggested stopping points and prompts:

- After reading the section called Building a Playground on the second page, ask: "What are the steps to follow in building your own playground?"
- At the end of the book, ask: "What would *your* perfect playground look like?" Follow-up: "What steps would you take to get it built? Turn and talk about your ideas with a partner."

MINILESSON Text and Graphic Features

TEACH Explain to children that *Playground Fun!* includes words that are special colors or sizes. Sometimes the letters are very large. Sometimes the letters are a different color and next to a picture.

1. Focus on the title *Playground Fun!* to introduce how authors use letters that are different colors and sizes. Suggested language: "In the title *Playground Fun!,* the author made the letters very big. The letters in *Fun!* are different colors. The author made the letters this way so the title would look fun, just like the word."

> **MINILESSON PRINCIPLE**
>
> Think about why the author made the letters different colors and sizes.

2. Page through *Playground Fun!* with children to find other examples of words that are special colors and sizes. Then write the minilesson principle on chart paper. Guide children to see how the author can use colors and sizes to make some words stand out and to help readers understand what the page will be about. Explain to children that paying attention to these clues will help them understand and enjoy what they read.

SUMMARIZE AND APPLY Restate the minilesson principle. Explain to children that they can apply it to their independent reading. Suggested language: "When you read, think about why the author made the letters different colors and sizes."

GROUP SHARE Ask children to describe an example from their independent reading of letters that are different colors and sizes. Have them explain what the color and size tell about the words. Then have them explain why they think the author made the letters that color and size.

Whole-Group Lessons • **71**

Whole-Group Lessons

Luke Goes to Bat
Student Book, Lesson 17

Tiger Woods: Superstar in Golf and Life
Teacher's Edition, Lesson 17

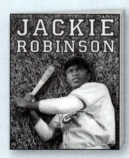

Jackie Robinson
Student Book, Lesson 17

▶ Luke Goes to Bat

INTERACTIVE READ-ALOUD/SHARED READING

Read aloud the story to children. Stop periodically for very brief discussion of it. Use the following suggested stopping points and prompts for quick group response, or give a specific prompt and have partners or threes turn and talk.

- After the first page, ask: "Where does this story take place?" Follow-up: "Why is it important that the story takes place there?"
- Just before Luke plays in the stickball game, ask: "What do you think will happen when Luke plays in the game? Why?"
- After Luke sees Jackie Robinson, say: "In your own words, tell what happens with Luke on the roof after the baseball game."
- At the end of the story, ask: "What lesson does Luke learn? Turn and talk with a partner about what you think."

MINILESSON Genre: Realistic Fiction

TEACH Display the minilesson principle on chart paper, and read it aloud to children. Tell children that some stories have events that could really happen and characters that are like real people.

1. Discuss the principle with children, using the events and characters from *Luke Goes to Bat*. Suggested language: "What important events happened in the story?" *(Luke watched and then played stickball; Luke went to a baseball game with his grandmother; Jackie Robinson visited Luke on a roof.)* Follow-up: "Which of those events could really happen?" *(stickball, going to the baseball game)*

2. Focus on Luke to help children understand how characters can be like real people. Suggested language: "Characters in made-up stories can say and do things like real people. Luke is a character in a story, but he acted like a real person. What did he do and say that was like a real person?" *(Luke played games. He liked baseball. He had dreams.)*

3. Use children's responses to help them notice story events that could really happen and characters who are like real people. Suggested language: "*Luke Goes to Bat* is a made-up story. Many of the story events, though, could really happen. The characters seemed real, too, because they acted like real people."

4. Work with children to identify other story events that could really happen or characters who acted like real people. Record children's ideas in a T-Map like the one shown here.

> **MINILESSON PRINCIPLE**
> Notice story events that could really happen and characters who are like real people.

Story Event or Character	How It Is Like Real Life

SUMMARIZE AND APPLY Restate the minilesson principle. Explain to children that they can apply it to their independent reading. Suggested language: "When you read a story, think about story events that could really happen and characters who are like real people."

GROUP SHARE Have children identify something in a story from independent reading that could really happen. Then have them talk about a character who is like a real person.

Lesson 17

▶ Tiger Woods: Superstar in Golf and Life

INTERACTIVE READ-ALOUD/SHARED READING

Read aloud the selection to children. Stop periodically for brief discussion. Use the following suggested stopping points and prompts:

- After Tiger becomes the Masters champion, ask: "What events helped Tiger become a great golfer at such a young age?"
- After reading about the Tiger Woods Foundation, ask: "Why did Tiger start the Tiger Woods Foundation?" Follow-up: "What does it do?"
- At the end, ask: "What sports do you like to play? How could you play as well as Tiger Woods? Turn and talk with a partner about your ideas."

MINILESSON Sequence of Events

TEACH Display the minilesson principle on chart paper, and read it aloud to children. Tell children they are going to notice the order of what happens to think about what a person did in his life.

1. Discuss the principle with children, using examples from *Tiger Woods: Superstar in Golf and Life*. Suggested language: "You can put the information you learned in *Tiger Woods* in order to tell what happened. What happened when Tiger was a toddler?" *(He learned the correct positions of the golf swing.)* Follow-up: "What happened later, when he was eight?" *(He won a junior championship.)*

> **MINILESSON PRINCIPLE**
>
> Notice the order of what happens to think about what a person did.

2. Explain to children that the order of what happens helps them to think about what a person did. Suggested language: "The author told about things that happened to Tiger before he turned twenty-one. Why is this information important?" *(Tiger already became a great golfer.)*

3. Work with children to notice the order of other things that happened in Tiger's life and discuss how those events explain what Tiger Woods did in his life. Write children's ideas in a Flow Chart.

SUMMARIZE AND APPLY Restate the minilesson principle. Explain to children that they should apply it to their independent reading. Suggested language: "When you read, notice the order of what happens. Think about how that order shows what a person did."

GROUP SHARE Have children retell the order of what happens to a person in a book.

▶ Jackie Robinson

INTERACTIVE READ-ALOUD/SHARED READING

Read aloud the book to children. Stop periodically for brief discussion. Use the following suggested stopping points and prompts:

- After reading the section called Into the Major League on the second page, ask: "How was Major League Baseball different before Jackie Robinson played in the major leagues?"
- At the end of the book, ask: "What did Jackie do after leaving baseball?" Follow-up: "Why do you think he chose that role? Turn and talk about your ideas with a partner."

MINILESSON Sequence of Events

TEACH Point out to children that the story *Jackie Robinson* is like *Tiger Woods: Superstar in Golf and Life*. Tell children that both books tell about the events in a real person's life.

1. Focus on dates and clue words that tell about order, such as *before that time* and *after that*. Show how those words help order what happens in a book. Suggested language: "*Jackie Robinson* included the dates when Jackie joined Major League Baseball and played in his last game. We can use those dates to figure out the order of when the events took place."

> **MINILESSON PRINCIPLE**
>
> Notice how dates and clue words help you think about the order of what happens.

2. Write the minilesson principle on chart paper. Then page through the book with children to find other examples of dates that tell about order. Guide children to see how dates can help them put events in order. Suggested language: "When did Jackie Robinson play his first game in the Major Leagues?" *(1947)* "What is another important date in Jackie Robinson's life?" *(September 30, 1956)* Follow-up: "Why are these dates important?" *(They show how long Jackie Robinson played in the Major Leagues.)*

3. Repeat the same type of questions, using order words. Explain to children that paying attention to these clues in a biography will help them understand more about the person's life.

SUMMARIZE AND APPLY Restate the minilesson principle. Explain to children that they can apply it to their independent reading. Suggested language: "When you read, notice how dates and clue words help you think about the order of what happens."

GROUP SHARE Ask children to point out two examples of dates or clue words that tell about order in a story they read for independent reading. Then have them tell how the dates and/or clue words helped them figure out the order of what happened.

Whole-Group Lessons • 73

Whole-Group Lessons

My Name Is Gabriela
Student Book, Lesson 18

Doctor Salk's Treasure
Teacher's Edition, Lesson 18

Poems About Reading and Writing
Student Book, Lesson 18

▶ **My Name Is Gabriela**

INTERACTIVE READ-ALOUD/SHARED READING

Read aloud the story to children. Stop periodically for very brief discussion. Use the following suggested stopping points and prompts for quick group response, or give a specific prompt and have partners or threes turn and talk.

- After the first page, ask: "Who is this story about?" Follow-up: "How and why did she get her name?"
- After Gabriela tells why she likes words such as *fluttering butterfly*, ask: "Why did Gabriela like words so much?"
- After Gabriela travels to the United States, ask: "How do you think Gabriela felt when she went to different countries? What makes you think so?"
- At the end of the story, ask: "How did Gabriela's love for words and stories change her life?" Follow-up: "What lessons can you learn from Gabriela's life? Turn and talk with your partner about what her story teaches you."

MINILESSON Understanding Characters

TEACH Display the minilesson principle on chart paper, and read it aloud to children. Tell children they are going to learn how to think about characters as they read.

1. Discuss the principle with children, using examples of characters from *My Name Is Gabriela*. Suggested language: "In *My Name Is Gabriela*, we met different people. Who were the people in the story?" (Gabriela; her mother and sister; Gabriela's friends Pedro, Ana, and Sofia)

2. Focus on Gabriela. Suggested language: "What did Gabriela do when she couldn't sleep?" (Gabriela imagined different things.) Follow-up: "What are some of the things she imagined?" (zebras with polka dots and rainbow-colored flowers)

3. Use children's responses to explain that what people do gives clues to what they are like. Suggested language: "The author used what Gabriela did (imagined interesting things) to show that Gabriela was creative."

4. Work with children to identify other examples from the book. Record children's ideas in a T-Map like the one shown here.

> **MINILESSON PRINCIPLE**
> Think about what characters do to understand what they are like.

What the Character Did	What the Character Was Like

SUMMARIZE AND APPLY Restate the minilesson principle. Explain to children that they can apply it to their independent reading. Suggested language: "When you read a story, think about what characters do to understand what they are like."

GROUP SHARE Have children identify something a character did in a story from their independent reading. Ask them to use it to explain what the character was like.

74 • Lesson 18

Lesson 18

▶ Doctor Salk's Treasure

INTERACTIVE READ-ALOUD/SHARED READING

Read aloud the selection to children. Stop periodically for brief discussion. Use the following suggested stopping points and prompts:

- After reading the second paragraph, ask: "Why was polio such a terrible disease?"
- After Dr. Salk finds out that the vaccine works, ask: "What is a *vaccine*? What clues from the story can you use to find out what it means?"
- At the end, ask: "Would you like to be a doctor? Why or why not? Turn and talk with a partner about what you think."

MINILESSON Cause and Effect

TEACH Display the minilesson principle on chart paper, and read it aloud to children. Tell children they are going to notice how one thing can make another thing happen. Explain that understanding why things happen will help them better understand what they read.

1. Discuss the principle with children, using an example from *Doctor Salk's Treasure*. Suggested language: "You learned that Dr. Salk won a prize in 1956. What happened to make him win the prize?" *(He made a medicine to protect children from polio.)*

> **MINILESSON PRINCIPLE**
>
> Think about how one thing makes other things happen.

2. Use children's responses to explain how to find how events are connected. Suggested language: "Dr. Salk made a new medicine. Because of the medicine, he won a prize. As you read, it is important to look for how one thing makes other things happen."

3. Work with children to find other events in the selection and what happens because of them. Record children's ideas in a T-Map labeled *What Happened?* and *Why?*

SUMMARIZE AND APPLY Restate the minilesson principle. Explain to children that they should apply it to their independent reading. Suggested language: "When you read, think about how one thing makes other things happen."

GROUP SHARE Have children share an example from their independent reading of one thing that made another thing happen.

▶ Poems About Reading and Writing

INTERACTIVE READ-ALOUD/SHARED READING

Read aloud the introduction and the poems to children. Stop periodically for brief discussion of the poems. Use the following suggested stopping points and prompts:

- After reading the poem "Share the Adventure," say: "The poem compares reading a book to riding on a seesaw. How are the two activities the same?"
- After reading all of the poems, ask: "What do you like about poems? What don't you like about them? Turn and talk about your ideas with a partner."

MINILESSON Genre: Poetry

TEACH Display the minilesson principle on chart paper, and read it aloud to children. Tell children they are going to think about how poems make pictures in their minds.

1. Ask children to close their eyes and listen as you reread the first four lines of "The Period." Then have them describe the picture in their minds. Suggested language: "What did you see in your mind when I read these lines?" *(Possible answer: I saw a heavy ball that would not move.)*

> **MINILESSON PRINCIPLE**
>
> Think about how words in a poem make pictures in your mind.

2. Ask children to close their eyes and listen as you reread the rest of the first stanza of "The Period." Next, ask volunteers to pretend they are a period and act out how a period acts in the poem. Then ask children to think about the picture these words made in their own minds. Suggested language: "How is the picture in your mind for this part of the poem like what the children acted out? How is it different?" *(Answers will vary.)*

3. Discuss with children the pictures they see in their minds after listening to "The Period" and "Keep a Poem in Your Pocket." Write their ideas in a T-Map labeled *Words in the Poem* and *Pictures in My Mind*.

SUMMARIZE AND APPLY Restate the minilesson principle. Explain to children that they should apply it to their independent reading. Suggested language: "When you read a poem, think about how the words make pictures in your mind. This will help you understand and enjoy the poem."

GROUP SHARE After reading a poem, have children describe or draw the picture that the words in the poem made in their mind.

Whole-Group Lessons • 75

Whole-Group Lessons

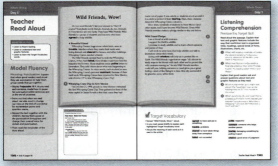

The Signmaker's Assistant
Student Book, Lesson 19

Wild Friends, Wow!
Teacher's Edition, Lesson 19

The Trouble with Signs
Student Book, Lesson 19

▶ The Signmaker's Assistant

INTERACTIVE READ-ALOUD/SHARED READING

Read aloud the story to children. Stop periodically for very brief discussion of it. Use the following suggested stopping points and prompts for quick group response, or give a specific prompt and have partners or threes turn and talk.

- After showing the delivery truck stopped at the *Ants Crossing* sign, ask: "What did Norman do while the signmaker was away? Why?"
- After the teacher tears down the *No School Today* sign, ask: "Why did the teacher tear down the sign?" Follow-up: "How did she feel when she did it? How do you know?"
- After Norman packs his bag, ask: "What words would you use to tell about Norman at the beginning and in the middle of the story?" Follow-up: "How did Norman change after he saw that the town was in danger without the signs?"
- At the end of the story, ask: "What lessons did Norman and the townspeople learn? Turn and talk with your partner about each lesson and why it is important."

MINILESSON Text and Graphic Features

TEACH Display the minilesson principle on chart paper, and read it aloud to children. Tell children they are going to learn how to notice important information in the art.

1. Guide children to use pictures to understand the story *The Signmaker's Assistant*. Display the page that shows Norman's trick signs on the bank, park, and toy store. Cover the text and ask: "What do you see in this picture?" *(The sign at the bank tells people to put money in the trash can. The sign in the park tells people to eat a hat. The sign at the toy store tells people to buy Norman a present.)*

MINILESSON PRINCIPLE

Notice important information in the art.

2. Tell children to think about the information in the art. "How did the pictures help you understand what was happening in the story?" *(The pictures showed what Norman was doing with the signs he placed around the town.)*
3. Use children's responses to explain that the clues in the pictures are important to understanding the story. Suggested language: "The author used the pictures to show that Norman was putting signs where they did not belong. The pictures showed that the signs tricked people. They also make you wonder why people did what the signs said because the signs were so silly."
4. Work with children to notice important information in art on other pages to better understand what happened in this story. Record children's ideas in a T-Map.

What the Art Shows	What It Says About the Story

SUMMARIZE AND APPLY Restate the minilesson principle. Explain to children that they can apply it to their independent reading. Suggested language: "When you read, notice important information in the art to help you better understand what is happening in the story."

GROUP SHARE Have children tell about the information in the art in a book they read for independent reading. Then ask them to explain what the information tells about their story.

76 • Lesson 19

Lesson 19

▶ Wild Friends, Wow!

INTERACTIVE READ-ALOUD/SHARED READING

Read aloud the selection to children. Stop periodically for brief discussion. Use the following suggested stopping points and prompts:

- After reading the first paragraph, ask: "What is Wild Friends? What do they do?"
- After reading the section A Beautiful Friend, ask: "What steps did Wild Friends take to save the whooping crane?"
- At the end, ask: "What would you do if there was an animal you wanted to save? Turn and talk with a partner about your ideas."

MINILESSON Genre: Informational Text

TEACH Display the minilesson principle on chart paper, and read it aloud. Explain to children that authors have different ways of organizing the ideas they want to share with readers. Display some examples of how ideas can be organized, including the following: order of events, how things are alike and how they are different, and what happened and why it happened.

1. Tell children they will think about how the author organized ideas in *Wild Friends, Wow!* Suggested language: "The first thing we read was that the places where Whooping Cranes built their homes were being used for buildings. This problem caused another event to happen. What happened when students learned about this problem?" *(The students tried to save the birds. They wrote letters and told other people about what was happening.)*

> **MINILESSON PRINCIPLE**
>
> Notice how the author organizes ideas.

2. Guide children to understand that the rest of *Wild Friends, Wow!* is organized in the same way. Suggested language: "What happened because the students wrote letters and told people about the birds?" *(Whooping Cranes have returned to New Mexico.)*

3. Revisit the list of ways authors can organize ideas that you introduced at the beginning of the lesson. Guide children to recognize that *Wild Friends, Wow!* uses the organization of what happened and why it happened.

SUMMARIZE AND APPLY Restate the minilesson principle. Explain to children that they should apply it to their independent reading. Suggested language: "When you read, notice how the author organizes ideas."

GROUP SHARE Have children identify how the author organized ideas in a book they read for independent reading. Then ask them to give examples of the clues that helped them decide how the author organized ideas.

▶ The Trouble with Signs

INTERACTIVE READ-ALOUD/SHARED READING

Read aloud the title, author, and cast of the play to children. Then read the play using two voices, or read it with a volunteer. Stop periodically for brief discussion. Use the following suggested stopping points and prompts:

- After Ben and Ana talk about the fork, ask: "What kind of fork is Ben talking about? What kind of fork is Ana talking about?" Follow-up: "Why is their talk about the fork funny?"
- After reading the play, ask: "Why do you think the author wrote this story as a play?" Follow-up: "How would the play be different if it were written as a regular story? Would it be better or worse? Turn and talk about your ideas with a partner."

MINILESSON Genre: Play

TEACH Display the minilesson principle on chart paper, and read it aloud. Explain to children that the author wrote *The Trouble with Signs* as a play. Tell children that a play has different parts that help tell the story.

1. Talk about the parts of a play with children. Suggested language: "A play has different parts. Like a book, a play has a title. What is the title of this play?" *(The Trouble with Signs)* Follow-up: "Unlike a book, a play has a cast. The cast is a list of the characters. Who is in the cast of this play?" *(Ana, Ben)*

> **MINILESSON PRINCIPLE**
>
> Readers notice the parts of a play.

2. Page through the play with children to note other features. Point out that the words that come after the characters' names are the words that the characters say. Guide children to see that the characters' words tell the story.

3. Help children notice that some of the words are set in parentheses. Suggested language: "The characters do not say these words. Instead, these words tell how the characters act when they read the words. They are called stage directions. What is an example of a stage direction from this play?" *(shaking his head)*

SUMMARIZE AND APPLY Restate the minilesson principle. Explain to children that they should apply it to their independent reading. Suggested language: "When you read a play, notice the parts of the play. This will help you understand and enjoy it."

GROUP SHARE After reading a play, have children name and tell about the parts of the play.

Whole-Group Lessons • 77

Whole-Group Lessons

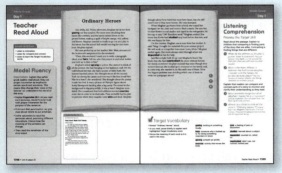

Dex: The Heart of a Hero
Student Book, Lesson 20

Ordinary Heroes
Teacher's Edition, Lesson 20

Heroes Then and Now
Student Book, Lesson 20

▶ Dex: The Heart of a Hero

INTERACTIVE READ-ALOUD/SHARED READING

Read aloud the story to children. Stop periodically for very brief discussion of it. Use the following suggested stopping points and prompts for quick group response, or give a specific prompt and have partners or threes turn and talk.

- After Dex decides he wants to be a superhero, ask: "Do you think Dex will become a superhero? What clues make you think the way you do?"
- After Dex tries on his superhero outfit for the first time, ask: "What steps did Dex take to become a superhero?"
- After Dex rescues Cleevis from the tree, ask: "Did Dex need special powers to do what he did?" Follow-up: "How has Dex *really* changed from the beginning of the story? Turn and talk with your partner about what the author is trying to say about what it takes to be a superhero."
- At the end of the story, ask: "What did the characters in this story learn?" Follow-up: "When have you learned the same lessons in your life?"

MINILESSON Compare and Contrast

TEACH Display the minilesson principle on chart paper, and read it aloud to children. Explain to children that it is important to think about how things are the same and how they are different as they read. Point out that they can think about how characters are the same and different to help them better understand the characters and why they behave the way they do.

1. Discuss the principle with children, using Dex and Cleevis from *Dex: The Heart of a Hero* as examples. Suggested language: "In *Dex: The Heart of a Hero*, Dex and Cleevis are two of the characters. What was the same about Dex and Cleevis?" *(They were animals. They hung around in the same neighborhood.)*

2. Talk about how Dex and Cleevis are different to show how to contrast. Suggested language: "How were Dex and Cleevis different?" *(Dex was a small dog and worked hard. Cleevis was a big, lazy cat.)*

3. Work with children to compare and contrast Dex and Cleevis. Record children's ideas in a Venn Diagram like the one shown here.

> **MINILESSON PRINCIPLE**
> Think about how characters are the same and how they are different.

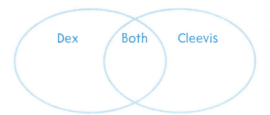

SUMMARIZE AND APPLY Restate the minilesson principle. Explain to children that they can apply it to their independent reading. Suggested language: "When you read, think about how characters are the same and how they are different."

GROUP SHARE Ask children to share how characters in a book they read were the same and how they were different.

78 • Lesson 20

Lesson 20

▶ Ordinary Heroes

INTERACTIVE READ-ALOUD/SHARED READING

Read aloud the story to children. Stop periodically for brief discussion. Use the following suggested stopping points and prompts:

- After Meghan gets her assignment, ask: "What problem does Meghan have in this story?"
- After Meghan thinks about Babe Ruth and Kristi Yamaguchi, ask: "What does Meghan think about Babe Ruth and Kristi Yamaguchi?" Follow-up: "Do you think that the athletes are heroes? Explain."
- At the end of the story, ask: "Who do you think Meghan will write about? What do you think she will say? Turn and talk with a partner about your ideas."

MINILESSON Compare and Contrast

TEACH Display the minilesson principle on chart paper, and read it aloud to children. Tell children they are going to learn how to think about the ways in which things in a story can be the same and different.

1. Discuss the principle with children, using *Ordinary Heroes* as an example. Guide children to think about how things are the same. Suggested language: "In *Ordinary Heroes*, you read about Babe Ruth and Kristi Yamaguchi. These two people were the same in some ways. How were they the same?" *(They were athletes. They had to exercise every day. They had to perform when they were sore and tired. They were Meghan's heroes.)*

> **MINILESSON PRINCIPLE**
>
> Think about how things are the same and how they are different.

2. Guide children to think about how things were different. Suggested language: "Babe Ruth and Kristi Yamaguchi were also different. In what ways were they different?" *(Babe Ruth was a man who played baseball. Kristi Yamaguchi was a young woman who figure skated.)*

3. Work with children to find things that are the same and things that are different about Meghan's mother and brother. Record children's ideas in a Venn Diagram.

SUMMARIZE AND APPLY Restate the minilesson principle. Explain to children that they should apply it to their independent reading. Suggested language: "When you read, think about how things are the same and how they are different."

GROUP SHARE Have children choose two characters, events, or other parts of a story they have read. Have them tell two ways the things were the same and two ways they were different.

▶ Heroes Then and Now

INTERACTIVE READ-ALOUD/SHARED READING

Read aloud the book to children. Stop periodically for brief discussion. Use the following suggested stopping points and prompts:

- After reading the introduction, ask: "What is a hero?" Follow-up: "Who are some of your heroes? Why? Turn and talk about your ideas with a partner."
- After looking at the chart of Olga Kohlberg and Muhammad Yunus, ask: "How are Olga Kohlberg and Muhammad Yunus the same? How are they different?" Follow-up: "How would you like to be like Kohlberg or Yunus?"

MINILESSON Genre: Informational Text

TEACH Explain to children that *Heroes Then and Now* is different from the other two stories they read this week because it gives information about real people and events. Display the minilesson principle on chart paper, and read it aloud. Explain to children that information books often include charts that give information.

1. Help children understand information in a chart by looking at the chart of Amelia Earhart and Ellen Ochoa. Suggested language: "What are the words in the arrows at the top of the columns?" *(Then, Now)* "Why is Amelia Earhart in the *Then* column and Ellen Ochoa in the *Now* column?" *(Earhart was a hero long ago and Ellen Ochoa is a hero today.)* Follow-up: "Why are Earhart and Ochoa side-by-side in the same chart?" *(The chart shows how two women who explored air and space were the same and different.)*

> **MINILESSON PRINCIPLE**
>
> Think about the information the author gives you in charts.

2. Discuss how charts give information. Suggested language: "This chart uses words and pictures to give information. What information does this chart help you understand?" *(how heroes today and in the past have done special things)* Help children understand that authors use charts to show information easily at a glance. Explain that reading charts for information will help them better understand what they read.

SUMMARIZE AND APPLY Restate the minilesson principle. Explain to children that they should apply it to their independent reading. Suggested language: "When you read, pay attention to charts to find out more about the information they give."

GROUP SHARE Ask children to share examples of charts in the books they chose for independent reading and tell about the information the charts give.

Whole-Group Lessons • 79

Whole-Group Lessons

Penguin Chick
Student Book, Lesson 21

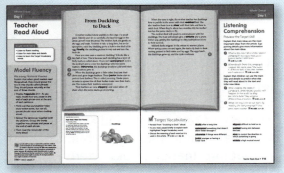

From Duckling to Duck
Teacher's Edition, Lesson 21

Animal Poems
Student Book, Lesson 21

▶ Penguin Chick

INTERACTIVE READ-ALOUD/SHARED READING

Read aloud the book to children. Stop periodically for very brief discussion of it. Use the following suggested stopping points and prompts for quick group response, or give a specific prompt and have partners or threes turn and talk.

- After the penguin mother leaves the rookery to feed, ask: "Why does the penguin father have to keep the egg warm?" Follow-up: "Do you think the penguin mother will get back before the egg hatches?"
- After the chick hatches and the penguin father trumpets across the ice, ask: "Why do you think the penguin father trumpet calls?" Follow-up: "Do you think he hopes the penguin mother will return soon? Why or why not?"
- At the end of the story, ask: "Could one penguin parent raise a chick alone? Turn and talk about your ideas with a partner."

MINILESSON Main Idea and Details

TEACH Display the minilesson principle on chart paper, and read it aloud to children. Tell children they are going to learn to think about how details give information about the main idea. Explain that the main idea is what a book or part of a book is mostly about.

1. Discuss the principle with children, using examples from *Penguin Chick*. Suggested language: "What is *Penguin Chick* mostly about?" *(how a penguin chick hatches and grows)* Explain to children that while the entire book is about penguin chicks, different parts of the book tell about different parts of the penguin's life. Each part of the book has a main idea, too.

2. Point out that one main idea is that a penguin mother lays an egg. Suggested language: "You learned that penguin mothers lay eggs, but they do not build nests. What details does the author give about this main idea?" *(There are no twigs or leaves. There is no grass or mud. There is only snow and ice.)*

3. Guide children to understand that another main idea in *Penguin Chick* is that it is the penguin father's job to protect the egg. Suggested language: "What information did the details tell about this main idea?" *(The penguin father holds the egg on his feet. It keeps the egg warm in a brood patch.)*

4. Help children identify other main ideas that the author shares about penguin chicks, such as the penguin mother's journey to the sea, how she feeds her chick, and how the chick grows. Record their ideas in a Web like the one shown here.

> **MINILESSON PRINCIPLE**
> Think about how details give information about the main idea.

SUMMARIZE AND APPLY Restate the minilesson principle. Then tell children to apply it to their independent reading. Suggested language: "When you read, think about how the details give information about the main idea."

GROUP SHARE Have children share a main idea from their independent reading book. Ask them to tell how the details gave more information about the main idea.

80 • Lesson 21

Lesson 21

▶ From Duckling to Duck

INTERACTIVE READ-ALOUD/SHARED READING

Read aloud the selection to children. Stop periodically for brief discussion. Use the following suggested stopping points and prompts:

- After the description of the newly hatched ducklings, ask: "How do you think a duckling feels?" Follow-up: "What words help you decide how the duckling would feel?"
- After the ducklings grow feathers and begin to preen, ask: "How has the duckling changed?" Follow-up: "How do you think having waterproof feathers will help a duckling?"
- At the end, ask: "Why do you think ducks like mallards have to fly to warmer places for the winter? Turn and talk about your ideas with a partner."

MINILESSON Main Idea and Details

TEACH Display the minilesson principle on chart paper, and read it aloud to children. Tell children they are going to learn how details give more information about the main idea.

1. Remind children that most books tell about one main idea. Suggested language: "In *From Duckling to Duck*, you read about mallard ducks. What did the author want you to learn about mallard ducklings?" *(how ducklings grow and change)*

> **MINILESSON PRINCIPLE**
> Think about how details give information about the main idea.

2. Talk with children about the details that give information about how the ducklings hatch and grow. Suggested language: *"From Duckling to Duck* began with the mother mallard laying her eggs near a pond. What did this tell you about ducklings?" *(They hatch from eggs.)* Follow-up: "What other details told you how ducklings grow and change?" *(When they hatch, they are covered in down. They grow feathers and begin to preen. They learn to swim and then to fly.)*
3. Record children's ideas in a Web. Help them tell how each detail gives more information about the main idea.

SUMMARIZE AND APPLY Restate the minilesson principle. Tell children to apply it to their independent reading. Suggested language: "When you read, think about how the details give more information about the main idea of the book."

GROUP SHARE Have children share the main idea of a book they read for independent reading. Then have them tell how the details gave more information about that main idea.

▶ Animal Poems

INTERACTIVE READ-ALOUD/SHARED READING

Read aloud the Readers' Theater to children. Stop periodically for brief discussion. Use the following suggested stopping points and prompts:

- After reading the first poem, ask: "What do you think the poet means when she asks, *Do you think ducks ever feel absurd speaking a language of just one word?"* Follow-up: "How would you answer her question?"
- At the end, ask: "Which poem did you like the most? Why is this poem your favorite? Turn and talk about your ideas with a partner."

MINILESSON Genre: Poetry

TEACH Explain that *Animal Poems* is different from the other two stories that children read this week because it is a Readers' Theater selection where the readers take turns introducing and reading poems. Tell children they will learn to think about the silly words and ideas in the poems.

1. Remind children that poems use words and the sounds of words to show ideas and feelings in different ways. Suggested language: "Many poets use silly words and ideas to help tell about their topic. What silly words are in the poem 'Quack?'" *(crackly-quick)* Follow up: "What silly ideas helped you to picture a duck's language in a new way?" *(Possible answers: the snap of teeth on a celery stick, speaking a language of just one word)*

> **MINILESSON PRINCIPLE**
> Think about the silly words and ideas in the poems.

2. Write the minilesson principle on chart paper, and read it aloud. Ask children to point out words and phrases in the remaining poems that helped them to see camels and other animals in a new way. Encourage them to tell why these words and phrases are special. Explain to children that paying attention to the words in a poem and how the words are used will help them to better understand and enjoy the poem.

SUMMARIZE AND APPLY Restate the minilesson principle. Tell children to apply it to their independent reading. Suggested language: "When you read a poem, remember to look for silly words and ideas that help you think about the poem's topic in a new way."

GROUP SHARE Ask children to share examples of silly words and ideas they found in poems they chose for independent reading.

Whole-Group Lessons • 81

Whole-Group Lessons

Gloria Who Might Be My Best Friend
Student Book, Lesson 22

The Middle Seat
Teacher's Edition, Lesson 22

How to Make a Kite
Student Book, Lesson 22

▶ Gloria Who Might Be My Best Friend

INTERACTIVE READ-ALOUD/SHARED READING

Read aloud the story to children. Stop periodically for very brief discussion of it. Use the following suggested stopping points and prompts for quick group response, or give a specific prompt and have partners or threes turn and talk.

- After Julian tells Gloria his name, ask: "Who do you think the girl is? What clues helped you decide?"
- After Gloria tells Julian that cartwheels take practice, ask: "How might Gloria know that cartwheels take practice?" Follow up: "Do you agree with Gloria? Why or why not?"
- After Gloria and Julian tie their wishes to the kite, ask: "What wishes would you tie onto a kite?"
- At the end, ask: "Which of Julian's wishes do you think will come true? Turn and talk about your ideas with a partner."

MINILESSON Understanding Characters

TEACH Display the minilesson principle on chart paper, and read it aloud to children. Tell children they are going to learn how to use what characters think or say to understand how they feel.

1. Discuss the principle with children, using examples from *Gloria Who Might Be My Best Friend*. Focus on Julian and his thoughts and words to guide children to understand how he feels. Suggested language: "In the beginning of the story, Julian was lonely, but he said that he didn't want a girl for a friend. Why didn't Julian want a girl for a friend?" *(He was worried that people would find out and tease him.)*

> **MINILESSON PRINCIPLE**
> Notice what characters think or say to understand how they feel.

2. Use children's responses to explain how what characters say and what they think are clues to understanding how they feel. Suggested language: "Julian was worried about what other people would think. What other story clues helped you figure out how Julian felt?" *(He wasn't sure where Newport was but he didn't tell Gloria. When he fell trying a cartwheel, he was worried that Gloria would laugh.)*

3. Ask children to recall the things that Julian thought and said that showed how he felt about Gloria. Record their ideas in a T-Map like the one shown here.

What Julian Thought or Said	How Julian Felt

4. Repeat the procedure, asking children to find examples of the things that Gloria thought and said that helped explain how she felt about her new home and how she felt about Julian.

SUMMARIZE AND APPLY Restate the minilesson principle. Then tell children to apply it to their independent reading. Suggested language: "When you read, think about what the characters think and say. Use these clues to help you understand how the characters feel."

GROUP SHARE Ask children to share what they learned about one character in a story they read for independent reading. Tell them to explain what the character thought or said that helped them understand how the character felt.

82 • Lesson 22

Lesson 22

▶ The Middle Seat

INTERACTIVE READ-ALOUD/SHARED READING

Read aloud the story to children. Stop periodically for brief discussion. Use the following suggested stopping points and prompts:

- After reading that Brendan copies everything Grace does, ask: "How do you feel when someone copies what you do?"
- After the author shares Grace's thoughts about Brendan's story, ask: "Why is Grace surprised to hear this story?"
- At the end of the story, ask: "How do Grace's feelings about her brother change in the story? Turn and talk about your ideas with a partner."

MINILESSON Understanding Characters

TEACH Display the minilesson principle on chart paper, and read it aloud to children. Tell children they are going to learn to use what characters in *The Middle Seat* say and do to understand what the characters are like.

1. Have children recall what Grace thought at the beginning of the story. Suggested language: "In *The Middle Seat*, you learned that Grace had problems with her little brother Brendan. How did Grace's thoughts help you understand how she felt?" (*Grace used words like* stuck *and* miserable *to tell how she felt about being next to Brendan.*)

> **MINILESSON PRINCIPLE**
>
> Think about what characters say and do to understand what they are like.

2. Point out that what characters do are also clues to understanding what they are like. Suggested language: "Think about the way Grace acted when Brendan wanted to tell her about what happened at school. What did this tell you about Grace?" (*Grace did not always treat her brother kindly.*)

3. Next, ask children to find clues that show that Grace was actually a kind and caring person. Write their ideas in a T-Map labeled *What Grace Said* and *What Grace Did*.

SUMMARIZE AND APPLY Restate the minilesson principle. Tell children to apply it to their independent reading. Suggested language: "When you read, think about what the characters say and do. Use what the characters say and do to help you understand what they are like."

GROUP SHARE Have children choose a character from their independent reading and tell what the character said and did. Then have them tell how these clues helped them understand what the character was like.

▶ How to Make a Kite

INTERACTIVE READ-ALOUD/SHARED READING

Read aloud the book to children. Stop periodically for brief discussion. Use the following suggested stopping points and prompts:

- After reading the Materials section, ask: "What does the information in the Materials box tell you?"
- After reading Step 2, ask: "What could you do if you didn't understand the directions for this step?"
- At the end, ask: "Do you think you could follow these directions to make a kite? Why or why not? Turn and talk about your ideas with a partner."

MINILESSON Genre: Informational Text

TEACH Explain to children that *How to Make a Kite* gives information about how to make something. Write the minilesson principle on chart paper. Tell children they will learn to notice how the author explains how to make or do something in an informational book.

1. Focus on the selection headings. Suggested language: "An information book that tells how to make something includes a list of materials and step-by-step instructions for what to do. Why do you think the materials are listed first?" (*The materials are listed first so that you can gather or make sure you have all the materials before you begin.*)

> **MINILESSON PRINCIPLE**
>
> Notice how the author explains how to do or make something.

2. Page through the book with children, pointing out the numbered steps in the instructions and the illustrations that go with each step. Guide children to notice that the author tells each step in order. Ask what might happen if the steps were told out of order. Suggested language: "What might happen if the steps were told in a different order?" (*The directions wouldn't work.*) Then ask children to tell how the illustrations help to support or explain the instructions.

SUMMARIZE AND APPLY Restate the minilesson principle. Tell children to apply it to their independent reading. Suggested language: "When you read an information book, notice how the author explains how to do or make something."

GROUP SHARE Ask children to share an example from their reading that told them how to make or do something. Have children tell what the author did to make the instructions easier to understand.

Whole-Group Lessons • 83

Whole-Group Lessons

The Goat in the Rug
Student Book, Lesson 23

Nothing But a Quilt
Teacher's Edition, Lesson 23

Basket Weaving
Student Book, Lesson 23

▶ The Goat in the Rug

INTERACTIVE READ-ALOUD/SHARED READING

Read aloud the story to children. Stop periodically for very brief discussion of it. Use the following suggested stopping points and prompts for quick group response, or give a specific prompt and have partners or threes turn and talk.

- After Geraldine tells about Glenmae sharpening the scissors, ask: "What do you think Glenmae will do with the scissors?"
- After Geraldine says that liking to eat plants got her into trouble, ask: "Why might liking to eat plants get Geraldine into trouble?" Follow-up: "What do you think will happen?"
- After Glenmae dyes some of the wool red, ask: "If Geraldine had not eaten Glenmae's plants, what part of a plant might she have used to dye the wool red?"
- At the end of the story, ask: "How long do you think it took Glenmae to weave the rug? What things in the story help you know? Turn and talk about your ideas with a partner."

MINILESSON Conclusions

TEACH Display the minilesson principle on chart paper, and read it aloud to children. Tell children they are going to learn to use clues in the story to figure out what characters are like.

1. Discuss the principle with children, using examples from *The Goat in the Rug*. Suggested language: "In *The Goat in the Rug*, Geraldine told the story. Think about the things that Geraldine said and did. What word would you use to describe Geraldine?" *(Possible answer: Geraldine was curious. She watched what Glenmae did.)*

2. Ask children to think about the things that Glenmae said and did. Suggested language: "How do you know that Glenmae liked Geraldine?" *(She talked to Geraldine. She let Geraldine follow her around. She didn't stay angry with Geraldine for long.)*

3. Tell children that when they read, they should use clues in the story to figure out what the characters are like. Suggested language: "Think about the clues in the story that told you more about Glenmae. What do you think Glenmae was like?"

4. As children answer the question, record their ideas about Glenmae in an Inference Map like the one shown below. Guide children to see that, in addition to being talented, Glenmae was a patient and hard-working person to put so much time and work into making a rug.

> **MINILESSON PRINCIPLE**
> Use clues to figure out what characters are like.

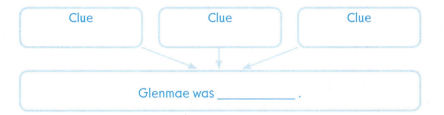

SUMMARIZE AND APPLY Restate the minilesson principle. Then tell children to apply it to their independent reading. Suggested language: "When you read a story, use clues in the story to help you figure out what a character is like. Look for things that the character says and does to help you decide."

GROUP SHARE Have children choose a character from a story they read for independent reading. Have them tell what story clues they used to decide what the character was like.

84 • Lesson 23

Lesson 23

▶ Nothing But a Quilt

INTERACTIVE READ-ALOUD/SHARED READING

Read aloud the selection to children. Stop periodically for brief discussion. Use the following suggested stopping points and prompts:

- After reading that this way of quilting was invented by African slaves, ask: "What would a quilt made out of scraps of fabric look like?" Follow-up: "What designs might it have?"
- After reading about the Milky Way and memory quilts, ask: "What ideas for designs might you have if you use things that happen around you or things in nature?"
- At the end, ask: "How are the Gee's Bend quilts like Navajo rugs? How are they different?"

MINILESSON Conclusions

TEACH Display the minilesson principle on chart paper, and read it aloud to children. Tell children that they are going to learn how to figure out some of the things an author means but does not tell.

1. Explain to children that authors do not always tell you everything. Sometimes you must figure out things on your own. Then say: "In *Nothing But a Quilt*, the author called the quilters of Gee's Bend artists. What do you know about artists?" *(Possible answer: They are creative. They make beautiful things.)*

> **MINILESSON PRINCIPLE**
>
> Think about what the author does not tell you but you can figure out on your own.

2. Point out to children that they can use what they know from their own experiences to figure out what an author does not tell them. Suggested language: "Think about what you know about quilts and artists. What can you figure out about the way the Gee's Bend quilts looked?" *(The quilts must have beautiful and interesting designs. Each quilt must look different from the others.)*

3. Work with children to identify other things they figured out that the author did not tell them. Use children's ideas to complete an Inference Map that tells how they figured out how the daughters and granddaughters of African slaves learned how to make the quilts.

SUMMARIZE AND APPLY Restate the minilesson principle. Tell children to apply it to their independent reading. Suggested language: "When you read, think about the things the author does not tell you that you were able to figure out on your own."

GROUP SHARE Have children share examples of things they were able to figure out on their own as they read.

▶ Basket Weaving

INTERACTIVE READ-ALOUD/SHARED READING

Read aloud the book to children. Stop periodically for brief discussion. Use the following suggested stopping points and prompts:

- After reading A Texas Tradition, ask: "What are some of the ways in which you and your family use baskets?"
- After reading Gathering Materials, ask: "Where do the basket weavers get their materials?"
- At the end of *Basket Weaving*, ask: "How is *Basket Weaving* the same as *The Goat in the Rug* and *Nothing But a Quilt*? How is it different? Turn and talk about your ideas with a partner."

MINILESSON Text and Graphic Features

TEACH Explain to children that *Basket Weaving* is similar to the other two stories they read this week because it talks about a craft that has been taught and passed down for many, many years.

1. Focus on *Basket Weaving* to introduce some of the special ways the author shares information. Point out to children the headings that go with each section. Suggested language: "*Basket Weaving* has three headings. What does each heading tell about the words that follow it?" *(what the topic of that part will be)*

> **MINILESSON PRINCIPLE**
>
> Notice special ways the author shares information.

2. Point out to children that authors also use photographs to share information. Suggested language: "What information did you learn from the photos? What information did the words next to the photos tell?" *(The photos helped me see what the baskets looked like, and the words next to them told about what the photos showed.)*

3. Write the minilesson principle on chart paper, and read it aloud. Guide children to explain the important information they got from the words and pictures in *Basket Weaving*. Explain to children that they will better understand what they read if they use special parts of a book such as headings, photos, and words that tell about photos to find important information.

SUMMARIZE AND APPLY Restate the minilesson principle. Tell children to apply it to their independent reading. Suggested language: "When you read, look for special ways the author shares information. Remember to look at the headings, photos, and the words next to them."

GROUP SHARE Ask children to tell about the special ways the author shared information in books they read independently.

Whole-Group Lessons • **85**

Whole-Group Lessons

Half-Chicken
Student Book, Lesson 24

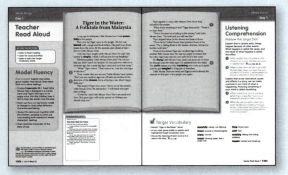

*Tiger in the Water:
A Folktale from Malaysia*
Teacher's Edition, Lesson 24

The Lion and the Mouse
Student Book, Lesson 24

▶ Half-Chicken

INTERACTIVE READ-ALOUD/SHARED READING

Read aloud the story to children. Stop periodically for very brief discussion of it. Use the following suggested stopping points and prompts for quick group response, or give a specific prompt and have partners or threes turn and talk.

- After learning what the thirteenth chick looked like, ask: "How do you think the other chickens acted when they saw the last chick?"
- After reading that the chick was the center of attention, ask: "What does it mean to be the center of attention?" Follow-up: "How can you use what you know about being the center of attention to figure out what the word *vain* means?"
- After Half-Chicken helps the wind, say: "Think about the things that Half-Chicken does. How does this help you know what Half-Chicken is like?"
- At the end, ask: "Why do you think the fire, the water, and the wind all helped Half-Chicken? Turn and talk about your ideas with a partner."

MINILESSON Cause and Effect

TEACH Display the minilesson principle on chart paper, and read it aloud to children. Tell children they are going to learn to think about what happens in a story and why.

1. Discuss the principle with children, using examples from *Half-Chicken*. Suggested language: "The story said that the chicks were running here and there, but the hen could not chase them because she needed to sit on the last egg. Why couldn't the hen chase her chicks?" *(The last egg had not hatched, and she needed to sit on it.)*
2. Tell children that when they read, they should think about what happens in a story and why. Suggested language: "Thinking about what happens in a story and why can help you better understand a story. Why did the stream need help?" *(Some branches were blocking its way.)*
3. Remind children that Half-Chicken also met a small fire along the way to Mexico City. Help children explain why the fire was almost out. Record their ideas in a T-Map like the one shown here. Help children name other events in the story and tell why the events happened.

> **MINILESSON PRINCIPLE**
> Think about what happens in a story and why.

What Happened	Why It Happened

SUMMARIZE AND APPLY Restate the minilesson principle. Then tell children to apply it to their independent reading. Suggested language: "When you read a story, think about what happens in the story and then think about why it happened."

GROUP SHARE Have children choose a story event from their independent reading to share. Ask them to tell why this event happened.

Lesson 24

▶ Tiger in the Water: A Folktale from Malaysia

INTERACTIVE READ-ALOUD/SHARED READING

Read aloud the story to children. Stop periodically for brief discussion. Use the following suggested stopping points and prompts:

- After Little Mouse Deer asks Tiger to carry him to the stream, ask: "What is a Mouse Deer? Do you think it is more like a mouse or more like a deer? Why?"
- After Little Mouse Deer tells Tiger that the other tiger is in the stream, ask: "What do you think Tiger will see when he looks in the water?"
- At the end of the story, say: "How do you feel about the way Little Mouse Deer tricked Tiger? Turn and talk about your ideas with a partner."

MINILESSON Cause and Effect

TEACH Display the minilesson principle on chart paper, and read it aloud to children. Tell children they are going to think about what happens in a story and why it happens.

1. Remind children that one thing in a story often makes another thing happen. Suggested language: "In the story *Tiger in the Water*, why were all the animals in the jungle afraid?" *(A tiger had come to the jungle.)*

2. Focus on what happened when Tiger caught Little Mouse Deer. Suggested language: "Why did Tiger say he was going to eat Little Mouse Deer?" *(Tiger said his tummy was empty. He was hungry.)*

3. Work with children to name other story events and why they happened. Record their ideas in a T-Map labeled *What Happened* and *Why It Happened*.

> **MINILESSON PRINCIPLE**
>
> Think about what happens in a story and why.

SUMMARIZE AND APPLY Restate the minilesson principle. Tell children to apply it to their independent reading. Suggested language: "When you read, think about what happens in a story and why."

GROUP SHARE Have children share events from their independent reading. Ask them to tell what happened in the story and why it happened.

▶ The Lion and the Mouse

INTERACTIVE READ-ALOUD/SHARED READING

Read aloud the story to children. Stop periodically for brief discussion. Use the following suggested stopping points and prompts:

- After the mouse asks the lion not to eat him, ask: "Does this story remind you of another story you know? How are the stories the same? How are they different?"
- After the lion notices the empty camp, ask: "Who do you think the camp belongs to?" Follow-up: "Why do you think the camp is empty?"
- At the end, ask: "How is the way the story ends like the story *Half-Chicken?* Turn and talk about your ideas with a partner."

MINILESSON Genre: Fable

TEACH Display the minilesson on chart paper, and read it aloud. Explain to children that the story *The Lion and the Mouse* is a fable. Tell them that a fable is a kind of story that teaches a lesson. Tell children that they are going to think about the lesson a character learns in this story.

1. Tell children that the lesson that a character learns is often shown by how the character changes. Suggested language: "In *The Lion and the Mouse*, the lion's feelings about the mouse changed from the beginning of the story to the end. How did the lion's feelings change?" *(In the beginning, he didn't think the mouse was useful. At the end, he learned that the mouse could help him.)*

> **MINILESSON PRINCIPLE**
>
> Think about the lesson that a character learns in a story.

2. Review the story events with children. Suggested language: "The lion learned the lesson because in the beginning of the story, he laughed at the idea of a mouse helping him. At the end of the story, the mouse was a great help to the lion, and the lion was grateful to the mouse. What lesson did the lion learn?" *(Little friends can turn out to be great friends.)*

3. Explain to children that the lesson a character learns is also a lesson for everyone who reads the story. Encourage children to tell how this lesson might help them in their own lives.

SUMMARIZE AND APPLY Restate the minilesson principle. Tell children to apply it to their independent reading. Suggested language: "When you read a story, think about the lesson that a character learns."

GROUP SHARE Ask children to share stories they read independently. Ask them to tell about the lesson a character in a story learned.

Whole-Group Lessons • **87**

Whole-Group Lessons

How Groundhog's Garden Grew
Student Book, Lesson 25

An Apple a Day
Teacher's Edition, Lesson 25

Super Soil
Student Book, Lesson 25

▶ How Groundhog's Garden Grew

INTERACTIVE READ-ALOUD/SHARED READING

Read aloud the story to children. Stop periodically for very brief discussion of it. Use the following suggested stopping points and prompts for quick group response, or give a specific prompt and have partners or threes turn and talk.

- After the animals collect seeds from inside peppers, cantaloupes, and cucumbers, ask: "Why are the animals collecting seeds?" Follow-up: "What will they do with them?"
- After Squirrel wakes Groundhog and tells him it's planting time, ask: "How long has it been since the animals first collected the seeds? How can you tell?"
- After Squirrel explains why some plants need to be planted in the back, with poles, or far apart, ask: "How would you plan a garden using Squirrel's advice?"
- At the end of the story, ask: "How do you think Groundhog feels at the end of the story?" Follow-up: "If you were Groundhog, would you share your garden harvest?"

MINILESSON Sequence of Events

TEACH Display the minilesson principle on chart paper, and read it aloud to children. Tell children they are going to learn how to think about the order of events to understand what happens in a story.

1. Discuss the principle with children, using events from *How Groundhog's Garden Grew*. Suggested language: "In the story *How Groundhog's Garden Grew*, things happen in order. Let's look at the very beginning of the story. What happened first?" *(Squirrel scolded Groundhog for eating his neighbor's garden and suggested he plant his own garden.)*

2. Focus on what happened when Squirrel suggested that Groundhog plant his own garden. Suggested language: "Groundhog admitted that he didn't know how to plant a garden. What did Squirrel do next?" *(She said she would show Groundhog how to plant a garden.)*

3. Use children's responses to explain how authors put events in an order that makes sense. Suggested language: "The author told what happened first and then told what happened next. When you think about the order in which things happen, it helps you understand the story."

4. Work with children to list the most important events from the whole story in order. Record children's ideas in a Flow Chart like the one shown here.

> **MINILESSON PRINCIPLE**
> Think about the order of events to understand what happens.

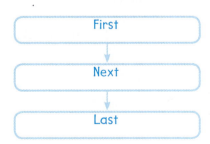

SUMMARIZE AND APPLY Restate the minilesson principle. Explain to children that they can apply it to their independent reading. Suggested language: "When you read a story, think about the order of events to understand what happens."

GROUP SHARE Have children share the order of events in a story from their independent reading. Ask them to tell what happened first, next, and last.

Lesson 25

▶ An Apple a Day

INTERACTIVE READ-ALOUD/SHARED READING

Read aloud the story to children. Stop periodically for brief discussion. Use the following suggested stopping points and prompts:

- After reading the first paragraph, say: "The author said that John Chapman often wore a coffee-sack shirt, a tin pot on his head, and no shoes. What can you tell about John Chapman from this information?"
- After learning that Chapman returned to Pennsylvania for more seeds, ask: "Why didn't John Chapman get seeds from the small apple trees he grew?"
- At the end of the story, ask: "Do you think what John Chapman did was important? Why or why not? Turn and talk about your ideas with a partner."

MINILESSON Sequence of Events

TEACH Display the minilesson principle on chart paper, and read it aloud to children. Tell children they are going to learn to think about the order of events to understand what happens in a story.

1. Discuss why it is important for authors to tell story events in order. Explain that if they did not, the story would not make sense. Then say: "In *An Apple a Day*, the author said that people began to settle the western part of the United States in the early 1800s. Why is it important to know that this event happened first?" *(It helps you understand why John Chapman wanted to plant seeds in Ohio.)*

> **MINILESSON PRINCIPLE**
>
> Think about the order of events to understand what happens.

2. Point out to children that clue words can help tell the order in which things happen. Suggested language: "What happened *after* a year or so when John Chapman had small apple trees to sell?" *(John Chapman sold or traded the trees. Then he went back to Pennsylvania to get more seeds.)*

3. Work with children to retell the events in *An Apple a Day*. Use a Flow Chart to record children's ideas and help them tell what John Chapman did first, next, and last.

SUMMARIZE AND APPLY Restate the minilesson principle. Tell children to apply it to their independent reading. Suggested language: "When you read, think about the order of events to understand what happens. Think about what happens first, next, and last."

GROUP SHARE Have children share the order of some events from a book they read for independent reading. Have them tell what happened first, next, and last.

▶ Super Soil

INTERACTIVE READ-ALOUD/SHARED READING

Read aloud the book to children. Stop periodically for brief discussion. Use the following suggested stopping points and prompts:

- After reading the introduction, ask: "What makes up soil?"
- After reading that humus soil is good for crops, ask: "Why is soil with humus best for crops?"
- At the end, ask: "How is the soil needed for growing crops different from the soil found in the desert? Turn and talk about your ideas with a partner."

MINILESSON Genre: Informational Text

TEACH Display the minilesson principle on chart paper, and read it aloud. Explain to children that the selection *Super Soil* is an information book. It gives real information about one topic.

1. Remind children that the author of an information book can share information in many ways. Suggested language: "The title, *Super Soil,* named the topic of the book. What information did the words by the picture on the second page give?" *(They told more about the picture. They told how the corn in the picture needs soil with a lot of humus to grow.)*

> **MINILESSON PRINCIPLE**
>
> Notice how the information in charts tells more about the topic.

2. Have children look at the chart. Guide them to notice that the chart gives more information that tells about the topic. It also shows the information in a way that makes it easy to understand and to compare. Suggested language: "What information does the chart give about the topic of soil?" *(It shows that there are different kinds of soil, and it tells how the types are different.)*

SUMMARIZE AND APPLY Restate the minilesson principle. Tell children to apply it to their independent reading. Suggested language: "When you read an information book, remember to notice the special ways an author gives more information, such as charts."

GROUP SHARE Ask children to name the topic they read about in a book they chose for independent reading. Have them share any charts the author included and explain how the charts gave more information about the topic.

Whole-Group Lessons • 89

Whole-Group Lessons

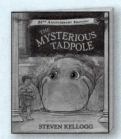

The Mysterious Tadpole
Student Book, Lesson 26

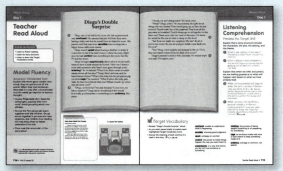

Diego's Double Surprise
Teacher's Edition, Lesson 26

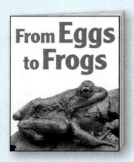

From Eggs to Frogs
Student Book, Lesson 26

▶ The Mysterious Tadpole

INTERACTIVE READ-ALOUD/SHARED READING

Read aloud the story to children. Stop periodically for very brief discussion of it. Use the following suggested stopping points and prompts for quick group response, or give a specific prompt and have partners or threes turn and talk.

- After Louis promises to take Alphonse to obedience school, ask: "What do you already know about how a tadpole becomes a frog?" Follow-up: "How is Alphonse different from normal tadpoles? Turn and talk about your ideas with a partner."
- After Louis says *But I can't put my friend in a cage!*, ask: "What is the problem?" Follow-up: "What do you think Louis will do to keep from sending Alphonse to the zoo?"
- At the end of the story, ask: "How is the end of the story the same as the beginning?" Follow-up: "If the story were to continue, what do you think would happen next?"

MINILESSON Story Structure

TEACH Display the minilesson principle on chart paper, and read it aloud to children. Tell children they are going to learn to think about where a story takes place and how it is important to what happens in the story.

1. Discuss the principle with children, using an example from *The Mysterious Tadpole*. Suggested language: "In *The Mysterious Tadpole,* Louis took Alphonse to live in a swimming pool instead of the zoo. Why was it important that the swimming pool was at a school?" *(It was important because the school was out for summer. It was a safe place to keep Alphonse for the summer.)*

2. Focus on when Alphonse retrieved the treasure chest from the harbor. Suggested language: "Ms. Seevers took Louis and Alphonse to a local harbor where a pirate ship sunk long ago. How did what they found in the harbor affect what happened?" *(They found a treasure chest. They used the money from the treasure chest to buy the parking lot and build a pool for Alphonse.)* Follow up: "Why was it important that the story took place near this harbor?" *(If this harbor wasn't nearby, they might never have found the treasure and had enough money to build the pool.)*

3. Use children's responses to complete a Story Map that shows the setting, characters, and plot. Make sure that children recognize how where the story took place was important to what happened.

> **MINILESSON PRINCIPLE**
> Think about where the story takes place and how it is important to what happens.

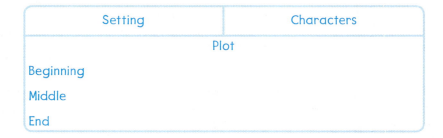

SUMMARIZE AND APPLY Restate the minilesson principle. Then tell children to apply it to their independent reading. Suggested language: "When you read, think about where the story takes place and how it is important to what happens."

GROUP SHARE Ask children to share an example from their independent reading of where the story took place and how it was important to what happened.

Lesson 26

▶ Diego's Double Surprise

INTERACTIVE READ-ALOUD/SHARED READING

Read aloud the story to children. Stop periodically for brief discussion of it. Use the following suggested stopping points and prompts:

- After the second paragraph, ask: "Why does Diego like having his own room?"
- After the fourth paragraph, ask: "What do you think the surprise will be?"
- At the end of the story, say: "Even though Diego will have his own room, his life will still be changed by the new twins. How do you think his life will change when the babies arrive? Turn and talk about your ideas with a partner."

MINILESSON Story Structure

TEACH Display the minilesson principle on chart paper, and read it aloud to children. Tell children they are going to learn to think about a story's problem and how the problem is solved.

1. Using *Diego's Double Surprise,* ask children to think about the main problem in the story. Suggested language: "In the story *Diego's Double Surprise,* we read about Diego. He was worried about how the new baby would change his life. Why did Diego think a new baby would be a problem?" *(He was worried about how they would share a room. He thought the baby might want to watch different television shows. He worried the baby might grow up and have more friends than him.)*

> **MINILESSON PRINCIPLE**
>
> Think about the problem in the story and how the characters solve it.

2. Talk with children about how the characters in the story solved the problem. Suggested language: "Diego's parents announced they were having twins. How did that change their plans to have the baby share a room with Diego?" *(The twins wouldn't be able to fit in a room with Diego, so his parents decided to build him a new room.)*

3. Display a Story Map, and have children help you complete it with information about the story, including the problem and how it was solved.

SUMMARIZE AND APPLY Restate the minilesson principle. Tell children to apply it to their independent reading. Suggested language: "When you read, think about the problem in the story and how the characters solve it."

GROUP SHARE Ask children to share an example from independent reading of how the characters solved the story's problem.

▶ From Eggs to Frogs

INTERACTIVE READ-ALOUD/SHARED READING

Read aloud the book to children. Stop periodically for brief discussion. Use the following suggested stopping points and prompts:

- After the first paragraph in From Tadpole to Frog, ask: "How are frogs and tadpoles different?"
- At the end, ask: "Why should people keep a frog in a fish tank instead of a cage? Turn and talk about your ideas with a partner."

MINILESSON Text and Graphic Features

TEACH Explain to children that the author of *From Eggs to Frogs* included special kinds of words and pictures to help them understand ideas.

1. Point out to children that the author of *From Eggs to Frogs* included headings and a chart. Suggested language: "In *From Eggs to Frogs,* the author wrote headings to tell about each section. The author also used a chart to show the life cycle of a frog. How did the headings help you?" *(They told me what each section was about. They told me where I could find different kinds of information.)* Follow-up: "How did the chart help you?" *(It showed me pictures of how a frog grows and changes. It included extra information.)*

> **MINILESSON PRINCIPLE**
>
> Notice the special ways the author helps you understand ideas.

2. Write the minilesson principle on chart paper. Help children to understand that authors include special kinds of words and pictures to help readers understand ideas. Explain to children that paying attention to the special ways an author gives information will help them understand what they read.

SUMMARIZE AND APPLY Restate the minilesson principle. Tell children to apply it to their independent reading. Suggested language: "When you read, think about the special ways the author helps you understand ideas."

GROUP SHARE Ask children to tell different ways the author helped them understand ideas in a book they read for independent reading.

Whole-Group Lessons • **91**

Whole-Group Lessons

The Dog That Dug for Dinosaurs
Student Book, Lesson 27

Epperson's Icicle
Teacher's Edition, Lesson 27

La Brea Tar Pits
Student Book, Lesson 27

▶ The Dog That Dug for Dinosaurs

INTERACTIVE READ-ALOUD/SHARED READING

Read aloud the story to children. Stop periodically for very brief discussion of it. Use the following suggested stopping points and prompts for quick group response, or give a specific prompt and have partners or threes turn and talk.

- After the explanation about how fossils form, ask: "Why do you think Mary and Tray find fossils near their home?"
- After the sentence about selling the fossils to tourists, say, "The word *souvenir* comes from a French word that means 'to remember.' How does a souvenir help you remember a place you've been? Turn and talk about your ideas with a partner."
- At the end of the story, ask: "How did Mary and Tray first learn to find fossils? How were they able to find so many fossils? Turn and talk about your ideas with a partner."

MINILESSON Fact and Opinion

TEACH Display the minilesson principle on chart paper, and read it aloud to children. Tell children they are going to learn how to notice the difference between words that can be proved and words that tell what the author thinks.

1. Discuss the principle with children, using example sentences from *The Dog That Dug for Dinosaurs*. Focus on the paragraph in which Mary and Tray find the pterodactyl. Suggested language: "In the story, the author said *Tray and Mary found a fossil that no one in England had ever found before*. Can these words be proved or are they what the author thinks? How do you know?" *(These words can be proved by looking in a history book to see if anyone in England found a pterodactyl fossil before.)*

> **MINILESSON PRINCIPLE**
> Notice that some of the author's words can be proved and some are what the author thinks.

2. After children demonstrate their understanding of fact, explain how to identify an opinion. Focus on the discovery of the ichthyosaur. Suggested language: "In the story, the author said *The amazing news spread about the gigantic fish lizard and the dog and little girl who had found it*. Which of these words might be something the author thinks but can't be proved? How do you know?" *(The word* amazing *is a clue that this is what the author thinks. Whether something is amazing cannot be proved. Some people might not think it is amazing.)* Follow-up: "What other words do you see on this page that show thoughts?" *(pretty, right, wrong, silly)*

3. Elicit from children additional examples from the story of words that can be proved and words that tell what the author thinks. Record children's ideas in a T-Map like the one shown here.

What Can Be Proved	What the Author Thinks

SUMMARIZE AND APPLY Restate the minilesson principle. Then tell children to apply it to their independent reading. Suggested language: "When you read, think about the author's words. Think about which words can be proved and which words are telling what the author thinks."

GROUP SHARE Ask children to share examples from their independent reading of words that can be proved and words that show what someone thinks. Tell them to explain how they knew the difference.

92 • Lesson 27

Lesson 27

▶ Epperson's Icicle

INTERACTIVE READ-ALOUD/SHARED READING

Read aloud the selection to children. Stop periodically for brief discussion. Use the following suggested stopping points and prompts:

- After the first paragraph, ask: "Why does the author call Frank Epperson *an accidental inventor*? Turn and talk about your ideas with a partner."
- After the third paragraph, ask: "Why is it important that these events took place in winter?"
- At the end, say: "Think about how Frank turned an accident into a popular treat. What lesson can you learn from this story? Turn and talk about your ideas with a partner."

MINILESSON Genre: Informational Text

TEACH Display the minilesson principle on chart paper, and read it aloud to children. Tell children they are going to learn to think about how the author makes information interesting.

1. Using examples from *Epperson's Icicle*, discuss with children what they found interesting in the story. Suggested language: "In *Epperson's Icicle*, we learned about how Frank Epperson accidentally invented the Popsicle. What information in this story did you think was interesting?" *(Answers will vary.)*

> **MINILESSON PRINCIPLE**
>
> Think about how the author makes information interesting.

2. Talk with children about why they found particular information interesting. Suggested language: "There are many different ways an author can make information interesting for the reader. Think about the information that you found interesting. Why did you think that information was interesting?" *(Answers will vary.)*

3. Help children to summarize the ways they think the author made information interesting for them, such as writing about a food they like or writing about a kid who did something exciting. Help them understand that writing about things that kids like is one way that authors make information interesting. List children's ideas on the board as they explain them.

SUMMARIZE AND APPLY Restate the minilesson principle. Tell children to apply it to their independent reading. Suggested language: "When you read, think about how the author made the information interesting."

GROUP SHARE Ask children to share an example from independent reading of something they found interesting.

▶ La Brea Tar Pits

INTERACTIVE READ-ALOUD/SHARED READING

Read aloud the book to children. Stop periodically for brief discussion. Use the following suggested stopping points and prompts:

- After the first paragraph, say: "Scientists remove lots of fossils from the La Brea Tar Pits. What do you know about fossils?"
- After the second paragraph, ask: "How do scientists know that Los Angeles was cooler and wetter than it is today?"
- At the end, ask: "Why are there so many fossils in the tar pits?"

MINILESSON Text and Graphic Features

TEACH Display the minilesson principle on chart paper, and read it aloud. Explain to children that *La Brea Tar Pits* is an information book that tells about a real place and gives information about real events in history.

1. Help children understand that information in a time line helps the reader understand a topic. Focus on the time line in *La Brea Tar Pits*. Suggested language: "The author of *La Brea Tar Pits* showed a time line at the end of the article. What did this time line show?" *(what La Brea was like from more than 100,000 years ago to today)*

> **MINILESSON PRINCIPLE**
>
> Think about how information in a time line helps you understand a topic.

2. Guide children in a discussion about how the information in a time line can help them to understand a topic better by showing information in a different way. Suggested language: "This time line shows how the area around the La Brea Tar Pits changed. It helps me to imagine what it would have been like a long time ago. If you needed to quickly find out something that happened at the La Brea Tar Pits, would you look at the time line or would you reread the whole article?"

SUMMARIZE AND APPLY Restate the minilesson principle. Tell children to apply it to their independent reading. Suggested language: "When you read, look for ways that information in a time line or another special feature can help you understand a topic."

GROUP SHARE Ask children to explain how a time line or another special feature in their independent reading helped them understand a topic.

Whole-Group Lessons • **93**

Whole-Group Lessons

Working in Space
Student Book, Lesson 28

Solving Problems with New Inventions
Teacher's Edition, Lesson 28

Space Poems
Student Book, Lesson 28

▶ Working in Space

INTERACTIVE READ-ALOUD/SHARED READING

Read aloud the book to children. Stop periodically for very brief discussion of it. Use the following suggested stopping points and prompts for quick group response, or give a specific prompt and have partners or threes turn and talk.

- After the Working in Space section, say: "In space, weightlessness causes everything to float around. Think about things you do every day. How would these things be different in space? Turn and talk about your ideas with a partner."
- After the Experiments on Astronauts section, ask: "Why don't astronauts use their bones and muscles very much in space?"
- After the Gloves and Ties section, ask: "Why do astronauts wear special spacesuits in space?" Follow-up: "What other special clothing has to be worn for doing a particular job? Why?"
- At the end of the story, ask: "Based on what you just read about how astronauts have to dress differently to work in space, how do you think life on Mars would be different from life on Earth?"

MINILESSON Text and Graphic Features

TEACH Display the minilesson principle on chart paper, and read it aloud to children. Tell children they are going to learn how to think about the special ways the author helps them understand ideas.

1. Discuss text and graphic features, using examples from *Working in Space*. Suggested language: "Each page of *Working in Space* has a special title in blue called a heading. What do these headings tell you?" *(These headings tell what each section is about.)*

2. Use children's responses to talk about how these headings are a special way the author helps the reader understand ideas. Suggested language: "The author included these headings to make the book easier for you to read. By reading the heading first, you know what to expect in the paragraphs. The headings help you understand the most important ideas."

3. Then lead children in a discussion about how the photographs help them understand the book. Guide children to recognize that these photographs help them see what the author is telling about, and this helps them to learn new things. Work with children to complete a T-Map that tells how words go with the photos in *Working in Space*.

> **MINILESSON PRINCIPLE**
> Think about the special ways the author helps you understand ideas.

What the Words Say	What the Pictures Show

SUMMARIZE AND APPLY Restate the minilesson principle. Then tell children to apply it to their independent reading. Suggested language: "When you read, think about the special ways an author helps you understand ideas."

GROUP SHARE Ask children to share an example in a book they read of a special way the author gave information. Have them explain how it helped them understand ideas in the book.

94 • Lesson 28

Lesson 28

▶ Solving Problems with New Inventions

INTERACTIVE READ-ALOUD/SHARED READING

Read aloud the selection to children. Stop periodically for brief discussion. Use the following suggested stopping points and prompts:

- After the second paragraph, ask: "Why do you think these inventions were created in the first place? Turn and talk about your ideas with a partner."
- After the paragraph about Cassidy Goldstein, ask: "How did Cassidy invent the Crayon Holder?"
- At the end, ask: "What is a problem that you'd like to solve with an invention? What would your invention be? Turn and talk about your ideas with a partner."

MINILESSON Compare and Contrast

TEACH Write the minilesson principle on chart paper, and read it aloud. Guide children to see how things in a story can be both alike and different. Explain to children that paying attention to how things are alike and different will help them understand what they read.

1. Focus on the inventions mentioned in the story to introduce how things are alike and how they are different. Suggested language: "In *Solving Problems with New Inventions,* the author talked about a few inventors. How were Cassidy Goldstein and Arnav Manchanda alike?" *(They were both children who had ideas about how to solve a problem.)*

> **MINILESSON PRINCIPLE**
>
> Think about how things are alike and how they are different.

2. Remind children that it is important to think about how things are alike and how they are different. Suggested language: "We talked about how Cassidy Goldstein and Arnav Manchanda were alike. How were their inventions different?" *(Cassidy's invention idea became a real thing that is now sold in stores. Arnav's invention was just an idea for the future. It is not real yet.)*

3. Work with children to create a Venn Diagram to show how things from the story are alike and different.

SUMMARIZE AND APPLY Restate the minilesson principle. Explain to children that they can apply it to their independent reading. Suggested language: "When you read, look for how things are alike and how they are different."

GROUP SHARE Ask children to share examples from their independent reading of two things that were alike and different.

▶ Space Poems

INTERACTIVE READ-ALOUD/SHARED READING

Read aloud the poems to children. Stop periodically for brief discussion. Use the following suggested stopping points and prompts:

- After reading "De Koven," say: "The title of this poem, "De Koven," is the name of a child. He is the speaker in the poem. What does De Koven want to do?"
- After reading "When I'm an Astronaut," ask: "Would you like to be an astronaut? Why or why not? Turn and talk about your ideas with a partner."
- After reading "Old Man Moon," ask: "What does the poet mean when she says that the Moon gets a birthday once a month?"

MINILESSON Genre: Poetry

TEACH Remind children that they have read three poems: "De Koven," "When I'm an Astronaut," and "Old Man Moon."

1. Read aloud the last four lines of "When I'm an Astronaut," emphasizing a feeling of excitement and adventure. Have children follow along. Then ask: "How do you feel when you hear these words?" *(happy, excited)*

> **MINILESSON PRINCIPLE**
>
> Think about how a poem makes you feel.

2. Help children notice other words that convey feelings. Read aloud the first two lines of "De Koven." Then ask: "In this poem, do these words have a silly sound or a serious sound?" *(silly)* "What other feelings do these words give you?" *(Possible answers: happy, greedy, excited)*

3. Ask children to share feelings they had about these poems. Prompt children to point out the words in the poems that helped create these feelings as you write the minilesson principle on chart paper. Explain to children that thinking about their feelings as they read a poem will help them enjoy it more.

SUMMARIZE AND APPLY Restate the minilesson principle. Tell children to apply it to their independent reading. Suggested language: "When you read a poem, think about how it makes you feel."

GROUP SHARE Ask children to share words or lines from poems they read independently and tell how they made them feel. Have children explain why they felt that way.

Whole-Group Lessons • 95

Whole-Group Lessons

Two of Everything
Student Book, Lesson 29

A Lesson in Happiness
Teacher's Edition, Lesson 29

Stone Soup
Student Book, Lesson 29

▶ Two of Everything

INTERACTIVE READ-ALOUD/SHARED READING

Read aloud the story to children. Stop periodically for very brief discussion of it. Use the following suggested stopping points and prompts for quick group response, or give a specific prompt and have partners or threes turn and talk.

- After the author explains that Mr. Haktak trades vegetables for goods, ask: "How does the author show that the Haktaks do not have much money?"
- After the Haktaks work late into the night doubling the coins, say: "This story is a folktale. What do you already know about folktales?" Follow-up: "What do you think will happen next?"
- After Mr. Haktak trips and falls into the pot, ask: "Why did the author use so many exclamation points and capital letters in this part of the story? What feeling does this show?"
- At the end of the story, ask: "Why were the Haktaks careful not to fall into the pot ever again? Turn and talk about your ideas with a partner."

MINILESSON Understanding Characters

TEACH Display the minilesson principle on chart paper, and read it aloud to children. Tell children they are going to learn how to think about how characters change.

1. Discuss the principle with children, using examples of characters from *Two of Everything*. Suggested language: "In the story *Two of Everything*, Mr. and Mrs. Haktak were the main characters. What were they like at the beginning of the story?" *(They were old and poor and living alone.)*

2. Focus on how things changed after Mr. Haktak found the pot. Suggested language: "How did things change for the Haktaks after Mr. Haktak found the pot?" *(They used the pot to get more money and items. Then, they accidentally fell in the pot and there were two of each of them.)*

3. Have children tell what Mr. and Mrs. Haktak were like at the end of the story. Suggested language: "What were Mr. and Mrs. Haktak like at the end of the story? How was this different from what they were like in the beginning?" *(They were friends with their doubles. They were richer and seemed happier than they were in the beginning of the story.)*

4. Use children's responses to the above questions to fill in a T-Map like the one shown here.

> **MINILESSON PRINCIPLE**
> Notice how characters change from the beginning of the story to the end.

Beginning	End

SUMMARIZE AND APPLY Restate the minilesson principle. Then tell children to apply it to their independent reading. Suggested language: "When you read, think about how the characters change in a story."

GROUP SHARE Ask children to share an example of a character who changed from a story they read independently. Have them tell how the character changed from the beginning to the end.

96 • Lesson 29

Lesson 29

▶ A Lesson in Happiness

INTERACTIVE READ-ALOUD/SHARED READING

Read aloud the story to children. Stop periodically for brief discussion. Use the following suggested stopping points and prompts:

- After the first paragraph, ask: "What clues tell you that this story is a folktale?"
- After Ela says she wants to see the boy's home, ask: "Why do you think Ela wants to see where this boy lives?" Follow-up: "What do you think will happen next?"
- At the end of the story, ask: "What is the lesson in this story? Turn and talk about your ideas with a partner."

MINILESSON Understanding Characters

TEACH Display the minilesson principle on chart paper, and read it aloud to children. Tell children they are going to learn to think about what characters do to understand what they are like.

1. Using the character Ela from *A Lesson in Happiness,* discuss with children that the way characters act gives clues about what they are like. Suggested language: "In the story *A Lesson in Happiness,* Ela was startled when a thin boy dressed in rags crossed her path. What happened next?" *(Ela helped the lost boy find his way home.)*

> **MINILESSON PRINCIPLE**
>
> Think about what characters do to understand what they are like.

2. Talk with children about Ela's reason for helping the lost boy find his way home. Suggested language: "Ela helped the boy because she felt sorry for him. Why did she feel sorry for him?" *(because she lived in a perfect kingdom and had never been lost)* Follow-up: "Think about what Ela did. What was she like?" *(kind, sensitive, understanding, helpful)*

3. Discuss with children characters' actions in stories they have read previously and how they show what the characters are like. Write their ideas in a T-Map labeled *What the Character Did* and *What the Character Was Like.*

SUMMARIZE AND APPLY Restate the minilesson principle. Tell children to apply it to their independent reading. Suggested language: "When you read, think about what characters do to help you understand what the characters are like."

GROUP SHARE Ask children to share an example from independent reading of something a character did and how it showed what the character was like.

▶ Stone Soup

INTERACTIVE READ-ALOUD/SHARED READING

Read aloud the story to children. Stop periodically for brief discussion. Use the following suggested stopping points and prompts:

- After the narrator says the villagers would not share with the stranger, ask: "Why do you think the villagers do not share with the stranger?"
- At the end of the story, ask: "How do the villagers end up sharing their food with the stranger?" Follow-up: "Why does the traveler's plan work? Turn and talk about your ideas with a partner."

MINILESSON Genre: Folktale

TEACH Remind children that they have read three stories this week: *Two of Everything, A Lesson in Happiness,* and *Stone Soup.* Explain to children that the stories have something in common—they are all folktales.

1. Focus on what the characters do in *Stone Soup* to introduce the idea that folktales often teach a lesson. Suggested language: "In *Stone Soup,* the villagers did not share their food with the traveler because he was a stranger. He then tricked them into sharing not just with him, but with each other, by making stone soup using food from all of them. The lesson is that sharing is good for everyone."

> **MINILESSON PRINCIPLE**
>
> Think about what the characters do and how the author is teaching you a lesson.

2. Write the minilesson principle on chart paper. Help children to understand that what the characters do supports the lesson the author is teaching. Have children retell the traveler's and villagers' actions in their own words and connect them to the story's lesson. Explain to children that figuring out what the characters in a story do and what they learn will help them understand the lesson.

3. Have children recall the lessons in the other folktales they read this week as you write them on chart paper. Ask children to turn and talk with a partner about which lesson they think is most important to learn.

SUMMARIZE AND APPLY Restate the minilesson principle. Tell children to apply it to their independent reading. Suggested language: "When you read, look for a lesson that the author is teaching."

GROUP SHARE Ask children to explain a lesson that the author teaches in a story they read for independent reading.

Whole-Group Lessons • 97

Whole-Group Lessons

Now & Ben
Student Book, Lesson 30

Godmothers and Goats
Teacher's Edition, Lesson 30

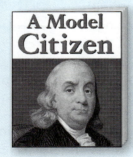

A Model Citizen
Student Book, Lesson 30

▶ Now & Ben

INTERACTIVE READ-ALOUD/SHARED READING

Read aloud the book to children. Stop periodically for very brief discussion of it. Use the following suggested stopping points and prompts for quick group response, or give a specific prompt and have partners or threes turn and talk.

- After the pairing about electricity, ask: "How would your life be different if there were no electricity?"
- After the pairing of Vitamin C and scurvy, ask: "Why do you think Ben Franklin came up with these ideas? Turn and talk with your partner about his reasons for inventing things."
- After the pairing about community establishments, ask: "Which of the services that Ben organized do you think is the most important to a community? Why?"
- At the end, say: "Think about the final question in the story: *Will his contributions help to form the future?* Turn and talk about your answer to this question with a partner."

MINILESSON Compare and Contrast

TEACH Display the minilesson principle on chart paper, and read it aloud to children. Tell children they are going to learn how to think about the ways in which things can be alike and different.

1. Discuss the principle with children, using *Now & Ben* as an example. Suggested language: "In *Now & Ben,* you learned about many of Ben Franklin's inventions and how some of them are still used today. What is one invention that is like something we use today?" *(Answers will vary. Accept any reasonable example from the story.)*

> **MINILESSON PRINCIPLE**
> Notice how things are alike and how they are different.

2. Then discuss how some of Ben Franklin's inventions are different from things we use today. Suggested language: "Some of Ben Franklin's inventions are different from things we use today. What is one of his inventions that has changed over time? How has it changed?" *(Answers will vary. Accept any reasonable example from the story.)*

3. Use children's responses to explain how to compare and contrast. Suggested language: "Think about how inventions have changed. Let's choose one from Ben's time and tell how it is the same as and different from what we use today." Record children's ideas in a Venn Diagram like the one shown here.

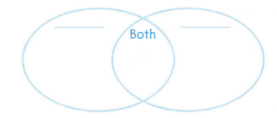

SUMMARIZE AND APPLY Restate the minilesson principle. Explain to children that they can apply it to their independent reading. Suggested language: "When you read, think about how things are alike and how they are different."

GROUP SHARE Have children compare and contrast two people, animals, things, or events they have read about. You may wish to have them tell about how two different books they read were alike and how they were different.

98 • Lesson 30

Lesson 30

▶ Godmothers and Goats

INTERACTIVE READ-ALOUD/SHARED READING

Read aloud the selection to children. Stop periodically for brief discussion. Use the following suggested stopping points and prompts:

- After the second paragraph, ask: "Why do people continue to read Charles Perrault's story today?"

- At the end, say: "The author says that people are still making up Cinderella stories today. If you were to make your own Cinderella story, which parts from the first one would you include? What would be new? Turn and talk about your ideas with a partner."

MINILESSON Compare and Contrast

TEACH Display the minilesson principle on chart paper, and read it aloud. Tell children they are going to look for ways that folktales are alike and different.

1. Focus on types of folktales to introduce how things are alike and how they are different. Suggested language: "In *Godmothers and Goats,* the author told us about different versions of the same story. The author explained that *Cinderella* is the same as and different from another story, *Little One-Eye, Little Two-Eyes, Little Three-Eyes.*"

> **MINILESSON PRINCIPLE**
>
> Notice how things are alike and how they are different.

2. Ask children to explain how these two stories are alike and how they are different. Suggested language: "What are some ways in which the character Cinderella is like the character Little Two-Eyes?" *(They both have a father who marries an unkind woman with two mean daughters.)* Follow-up: "How are their wishes different?" *(Cinderella wants to go to a ball. Little Two-Eyes wants food.)*

3. Guide children to choose another story that they all know. Have them name ways that *Cinderella* and this story are alike and different. Record children's ideas in a Venn Diagram.

SUMMARIZE AND APPLY Restate the minilesson principle. Explain to children that they can apply it to their independent reading. Suggested language: "When you read, look for how things are alike and how they are different."

GROUP SHARE Ask children to tell about the book they read for independent reading. Have them explain how things in the book and things in another book they've read were alike and different.

▶ A Model Citizen

INTERACTIVE READ-ALOUD/SHARED READING

Read aloud the book to children. Stop periodically for brief discussion. Use the following suggested stopping points and prompts:

- After the second paragraph, ask: "How does a public library make life better for people?"

- After reading the end, say: "The title is *A Model Citizen.* What does that mean?" Follow-up: "Why is Ben Franklin a model citizen? Turn and talk about your ideas with a partner."

MINILESSON Genre: Informational Text

TEACH Display the minilesson principle on chart paper, and read it aloud. Tell children they are going to think about the ideas in a book and decide how the ideas fit into their own lives and experiences.

1. Focus on the thirteen original colonies. Suggested language: "In *A Model Citizen,* the author told how the colonists asked Franklin to help them become free. Those thirteen colonies later became the United States of America. Knowing this history helps us understand why America is a free country today."

> **MINILESSON PRINCIPLE**
>
> Think about the ideas and why they are important to you.

2. Lead children in a discussion about why it is important to know about the history of their country. Suggested language: "You read that Benjamin Franklin started the first fire company. How would your life be different if this had not happened?" *(Possible answer: I would not be as safe.)* Have children continue to talk about what other histories might be important to them, such as a family history or local history.

SUMMARIZE AND APPLY Restate the minilesson principle. Tell children to apply it to their independent reading. Suggested language: "When you read, think about why the ideas are important to you."

GROUP SHARE Ask children to explain the ideas from the story they read for independent reading and why that information is important to them.

Whole-Group Lessons • **99**

Teacher's Notes

Teaching Genre

Genre instruction and repeated exposure to a variety of genres are essential components of any high-quality literacy program. Access to the tools children need to understand information in different genres will make them better readers. When children understand the characteristics of a variety of genres, they will be able to:

- gain an appreciation for a wide range of texts
- develop a common vocabulary for talking about texts
- begin reading texts with a set of expectations related to genre
- make evidence-based predictions
- develop preferences as readers
- understand purposes for reading and writing
- recognize the choices an author makes when writing
- compare and contrast texts
- think deeply about what they read

The pages in this section provide a framework for discussing genre with your students in an age-appropriate way. You can use the lists on the following pages to organize for genre discussion.

- **Genre Characteristics:** teach and review the salient features
- **Discussion Starters:** begin and maintain productive discussions
- **Comparing Texts:** encourage children to make connections across texts
- **Literature:** select *Journeys* literature for discussion

Fantasy	102	Realistic Fiction	106
Folktale	103	Poetry	107
Fable	104	Informational Text	108
Humorous Fiction	105	Biography	110

101

Fantasy

SUPPORT THINKING

DISCUSSION STARTERS During whole-group and small-group discussion, use questions to spark conversation about genre characteristics.

- Who are the characters in this story?
- What is [character name] like? What can he/she do that is special?
- What is happening in this story?
- What problem does [character name] have? How does he/she solve this problem?
- Where is this story happening? Is it a place that you would like to visit? Explain.
- Which parts of this story could not happen in real life?
- Which characters could not live in the real world? How do you know?
- Would you like to read more stories that are like [title]? Why or why not?

COMPARING TEXTS After children have read and listened to several fantasy stories, prompt them to compare stories and to recognize common characteristics. Use questions such as these:

- How are the characters in [title] and [title] the same?
- Which character would you rather be—[character name] or [character name]? Why?
- How is the setting in [title] like places in other stories you have read? How is it different?
- How is [title] the same as other stories you have read? How is it different?
- How is the ending of [title] different from the ending of [title]?

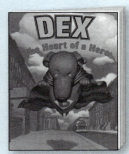 

Dex: The Heart of a Hero, Student Book, Lesson 20

How Groundhog's Garden Grew, Student Book, Lesson 25

102 • Teaching Genre: Fantasy

Genre Characteristics

A fantasy story is a made-up story that could not happen in real life.

Through repeated exposure to fantasy stories, children should learn to notice common genre characteristics, though they will not be expected to use all the technical labels. Use friendly language to help them understand the following concepts:

- **Author's Purpose:** to entertain
- **Characters:** the people or animals in a story; characters in fantasy stories often have special abilities
- **Characters' Actions/Qualities:** characters often have feelings like those of real people but can do amazing things; animals and objects may talk
- **Setting:** where and when the story takes place; often set in a different time or in a make-believe place
- **Plot:** what happens in the story; includes a problem, sometimes unrealistic events that happen as characters try to solve the problem, and an ending; the problem may be similar to problems in real life
- **Dialogue:** the words that characters say to each other; shows what characters are like and what they think of other characters
- **Theme/Message:** what the author is trying to say to readers

Journeys Literature

STUDENT BOOK
Dex: The Heart of a Hero
How Groundhog's Garden Grew
The Mysterious Tadpole

TEACHER'S EDITION READ-ALOUD
The Owl Hunt
Trouble in the Lily Garden

LEVELED READERS
Bee's Beautiful Garden N
Chipmunks Do What Chipmunks Do I
The Colors of Leaves I
The Giant Forest H
How the Leaves Got Their Colors K
Jason and the Space Creature K

Katy's Inventions N
Larry the Singing Chicken J
The Mysterious Superhero
Planet Zogo L
Rabbit's Garden L
Rabbit's Garden Troubles L
Superheroes Save the Day J
Superheroes to the Rescue
Two Heroes I

Folktale

Genre Characteristics

A folktale is a made-up story that was first told aloud to explain something or to teach a lesson. It has been told over and over for many years.

Through repeated exposure to folktales, children should learn to notice common genre characteristics, though they will not be expected to use all the technical labels. Use friendly language to help them understand the following concepts:

- **Author's Purpose:** to entertain; to teach a lesson
- **Characters:** the people or animals in a story; animals may talk and act like people; characters change or learn something throughout the story
- **Setting:** where and when the story takes place; usually set long ago in a specific place (often where the story originated)
- **Plot:** what happens in the story; includes a problem that characters face, events that happen as characters try to solve the problem, and an ending
- **Dialogue:** the words that characters say to each other
- **Theme/Message:** the lesson that the author wants to teach readers; often tells what a group of people believes; may tell a group's explanation for why things are the way they are

Journeys Literature

STUDENT BOOK
Half-Chicken
How Chipmunk Got His Stripes
Stone Soup
Two of Everything
Why Rabbits Have Short Tails

TEACHER'S EDITION READ-ALOUD
A Lesson in Happiness
On Thin Ice

Tiger in the Water: A Folktale from Malaysia

LEVELED READERS
Brer Rabbit at the Well I
Camel's Hump I
Coyote and the Rabbit M
Groundhog's New Home N
How Coyote Stole Fire K
How People Got Fire K
Mouse and Crocodile L
The Smart Mouse K
The Trick J
Uncle Rabbit N
Wali Dad's Gifts P

SUPPORT THINKING

DISCUSSION STARTERS During whole-group and small-group discussion, use questions to spark conversation about genre characteristics.

- Who are the characters in this story?
- What is [character name] like?
- What problem does [character name] have? How does [character name] solve the problem?
- Where is this story happening? What is the place like?
- What can you tell about [character name] by what he/she says?
- Which parts of this story could not happen in real life? Explain how you know.
- What happens to characters who are good? To characters who are bad?
- What does this story explain?
- What lesson can you learn by reading this story?
- What clues help you know that [title] is a folktale?

COMPARING TEXTS After children have read and listened to several folktales, prompt them to compare stories and to recognize common characteristics. Use questions such as these:

- How are the characters in [title] and [title] the same? How are they different?
- How is [title] the same as other stories you have read? How is it different?
- Think about the ending of [title]. How is this ending different from the ending of [title]?

How Chipmunk Got His Stripes, Student Book, Lesson 9

Half-Chicken, Student Book, Lesson 24

Teaching Genre: Folktale • 103

Fable

SUPPORT THINKING

DISCUSSION STARTERS During whole-group and small-group discussion, use questions to spark conversation about genre characteristics.

- Who are the characters in this story?
- What is [character name] like? How do you know?
- What problem does [character name] have?
- What does [character name] do to solve the problem?
- Where is this story happening?
- What can you tell about [character name] by what he/she says? What can you tell about [character name] from the pictures?
- What do other characters think of [character name]?
- What does [character name] learn?
- What is the lesson of the story?

COMPARING TEXTS After children have read and listened to several fables, prompt them to compare stories and to recognize common characteristics. Use questions such as these:

- How are the characters in [title] and [title] the same?
- How is [title] the same as other stories you have read?
- How are the lessons the characters learn in [title] and [title] the same?
- How is [title] different from another fable you have read?

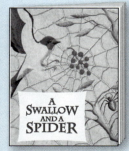

A Swallow and a Spider, Student Book, Lesson 4

The Lion and the Mouse, Student Book, Lesson 24

Genre Characteristics

A fable is a short, made-up story that teaches a lesson.

Through repeated exposure to fables, children should learn to notice common genre characteristics, though they will not be expected to use all the technical labels. Use friendly language to help them understand the following concepts:

- **Author's Purpose:** to entertain; to teach a lesson
- **Characters:** the people or animals in a story; characters in fables are often animals or objects that talk and act like people
- **Setting:** where and when the story takes place; could be a real or a make-believe place
- **Plot:** what happens in the story; includes a problem that characters face, what happens as characters try to solve the problem, and an ending; most events could not really happen
- **Dialogue:** the words that characters say to each other
- **Message/Moral:** the lesson characters learn from what happens in the story; the moral is sometimes stated at the end of the story

Journeys Literature

STUDENT BOOK
The Lion and the Mouse
A Swallow and a Spider

LEVELED READERS
Favorite Fables J

104 • Teaching Genre: Fable

Humorous Fiction

Genre Characteristics

Humorous fiction is a made-up story in which characters and events are meant to make readers laugh.

Through repeated exposure to humorous fiction, children should learn to notice common genre characteristics, though they will not be expected to use all the technical labels. Use friendly language to help them understand the following concepts:

- **Author's Purpose:** to entertain
- **Characters:** the people or animals in a story; characters in humorous fiction say and do funny things
- **Setting:** where and when the story happens; could be a real or a make-believe place
- **Plot:** what happens in the story; includes a problem that characters face, events that happen as characters try to solve the problem, and an ending; events may include a series of mishaps or accidents that add humor to the story
- **Dialogue:** the words that characters say to each other; characters' words may be funny or unexpected

Journeys Literature

STUDENT BOOK
Click, Clack, Moo: Cows That Type
Diary of a Spider
Officer Buckle and Gloria
The Signmaker's Assistant

LEVELED READERS
Aldo and Abby I
The Best Student J

Cub Saves the Day H
E-Mails from the Teacher N
Ferdinand Saves the Day N
Finding the Party K
Firedog! G
Flora the Fly Saves the Spiders J
Fly to the Rescue! J
Good Citizen J
Pay Attention! K

Sam Finds the Party K
The Smiths and Their Animals J
Too Many Signs! L
A Well-Trained Dog M
Zoo Party H

SUPPORT THINKING

DISCUSSION STARTERS During whole-group and small-group discussion, use questions to spark conversation about genre characteristics.

- Who are the characters in this story?
- What is happening in this story?
- What problem does [character name] have?
- What is funny about the way [character name] tries to solve the problem?
- What can you tell about [character name] by what he/she does?
- Where and when is this story happening?
- Which parts of the story could really happen? Which parts could not happen?
- What parts of the story do you think are funny?

COMPARING TEXTS After children have read and listened to several humorous fiction stories, prompt them to compare stories and to recognize common characteristics. Use questions such as these:

- How are the characters in [title] and [title] the same?
- How is [title] the same as other stories you have read? How is it different?
- Which story do you think is funnier—[title] or [title]? Which story would make a better movie? Explain.

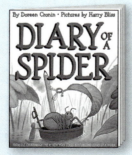

Diary of a Spider, Student Book, Lesson 4

The Signmaker's Assistant, Student Book, Lesson 19

Teaching Genre: Humorous Fiction • **105**

Realistic Fiction

SUPPORT THINKING

DISCUSSION STARTERS During whole-group and small-group discussion, use questions to spark conversation about genre characteristics.

- Who are the characters in this story?
- What is [character name] like?
- What clues help you learn about [character name]?
- What is happening in this story?
- What problem does [character name] have?
- How does [character name] solve the problem?
- Where is this story happening? How can you tell that the place could be real?
- When is this story happening?
- Which person in [title] makes you think about someone you know?
- How is the problem in this story like real problems you know about?

COMPARING TEXTS After children have read and listened to several realistic fiction stories, prompt them to compare stories and to recognize common characteristics. Use questions such as these:

- How are the characters in [title] and [title] the same?
- How is [title] the same as other stories you have read? How is it different?
- Which story seems more real—[title] or [title]? Explain.
- Would you like to read more stories like [title]? Why or why not?

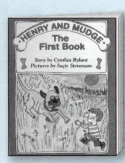

Henry and Mudge, Student Book, Lesson 1

Gloria Who Might Be My Best Friend, Student Book, Lesson 22

Genre Characteristics

Realistic fiction is a made-up story that could happen in real life.

Through repeated exposure to realistic fiction, children should learn to notice common genre characteristics, though they will not be expected to use all the technical labels. Use friendly language to help them understand the following concepts:

- **Author's Purpose:** to entertain
- **Characters:** the people or animals in a story; characters in realistic fiction might remind children of people they know
- **Setting:** where and when the story happens; could be based on a real place
- **Plot:** what happens in the story; includes a problem that characters face, events that happen as characters try to solve the problem, and an ending; problems and events are similar to those in real life
- **Dialogue:** the words that characters say to each other; shows what characters are like and what they think of other characters; characters talk like real people

Journeys Literature

STUDENT BOOK

Gloria Who Might Be My Best Friend
Henry and Mudge
Henry and Mudge Under the Yellow Moon
Luke Goes to Bat
Mr. Tanen's Tie Trouble
Teacher's Pet
The Ugly Vegetables
Violet's Music

TEACHER'S EDITION READ-ALOUD

Adventures at Scout Camp
A Better Way to Save
Diego's Double Surprise
Lester
The Middle Seat

Ordinary Heroes
The Perfect Pet
Rita Breaks the Rules

LEVELED READERS

Annie's Pictures **L**
The Bake Sale **K**
Ben and Sooty **H**
Billy, the Pet Bird **H**
Caty the Caterpillar **H**
The Community Garden **J**
Cross-Country Cousins **O**
Elena's Wish **J**
Every Kind of Wish **K**
Foster's Famous Farm **J**
Foster's Farm **J**
Grandma's Surprise **G**
The Kite Contest **I**
Lucy and Billy **L**

Luz and the Garden **J**
Ms. Hawkins and the Bake Sale **K**
The New Field **M**
Our Library **I**
A Pet That Fits **M**
A Real Band **G**
Rosa the Painter **J**
Sand Castle Contest **N**
The Summer of Baseball Parks **K**
Take Me Out to the Ballpark **K**
A Thousand Words **O**
The Town Auction **M**
What Can Rosa Paint? **J**
Where Is Gus-Gus? **L**
The Winning Hit **G**

106 • Teaching Genre: Realistic Fiction

Poetry

Genre Characteristics

Poetry is a piece of writing in which words are used to show feelings and ideas.

Through repeated exposure to poetry, children should learn to notice common genre characteristics, though they will not be expected to use all the technical labels. Use friendly language to help them understand the following concepts:

- **Author's Purpose:** to entertain; to express
- **Form:** includes traditional rhymes, songs, chants, free verse, and list poems
- **Shape:** poem may be shaped like the thing it describes
- **Rhyme:** to have the same ending sound; rhyming words can make a poem fun to read
- **Rhythm:** the beat of how the words are read; may be slow or fast
- **Repetition:** repeating of words, lines, or sounds to create rhythm or to make something stand out
- **Sensory Words:** words that describe how things look, feel, taste, smell, and sound
- **Repeated Readings:** can often help readers enjoy and understand a poem more

Journeys Literature

STUDENT BOOK
Animal Poems
Family Poetry
Poems About Reading and Writing
School Poems
Space Poems
Weather Poems

SUPPORT THINKING

DISCUSSION STARTERS During whole-group and small-group discussion, use questions to spark conversation about genre characteristics.

- What does this poem tell about?
- Which words in the poem rhyme?
- Which words in the poem help you picture something?
- Which words in the poem describe sounds? Which words describe smells? Which words describe tastes?
- Is the poem silly or serious? How do you know?
- Which sounds or words in the poem repeat? Why do you think the poet did this?
- How does the poem make you feel?

COMPARING TEXTS After children have read and listened to several poems, prompt them to compare poems and to recognize common characteristics. Use questions such as these:

- How are [title] and [title] the same? How are they different?
- How are the poems in [title] the same as other poems you have read?
- What is different about how [title] and [title] are shaped?

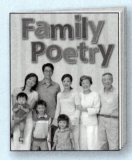 

Family Poetry, Student Book, Lesson 2

Poems About Reading and Writing, Student Book, Lesson 18

Teaching Genre: Poetry • **107**

Informational Text

SUPPORT THINKING

DISCUSSION STARTERS During whole-group and small-group discussion, use questions to spark conversation about genre characteristics.

- What is this book mostly about?
- Why did the author write this book? How do you know?
- How does the author use different kinds of type to help you see what is important?
- What information do you learn from the pictures?
- What does the author do to make the book interesting?
- How does the author organize information to help you understand what you are reading?
- How do you know that the information in the book is true?
- How does the author feel about the topic? How do you know?

COMPARING TEXTS After children have read and listened to several informational selections, prompt them to compare selections and to recognize common characteristics. Use questions such as these:

- Think about how the pictures are used in [title]. How are pictures used in a different way in [title]?
- How is the way the information is organized in [title] different from the way the information is organized in [title]?
- [Title] and [title] are both mostly about [topic]. Which book makes you want to read more about [topic]? Explain.
- How is [title] different from a fiction book about the same topic?

My Family, Student Book, Lesson 2

Penguin Chick, Student Book, Lesson 21

108 • Teaching Genre: Informational Text

Genre Characteristics

Informational text gives facts about real people, places, things, or events.

Through repeated exposure to informational text, children should learn to notice common genre characteristics, though they will not be expected to use all the technical labels. Use friendly language to help them understand the following concepts:

- **Author's Purpose:** to inform about a topic
- **Illustrations/Photographs:** accurately show the ideas being described to help readers understand them
- **Graphic Features:** pictures that help the reader understand information or show more about the topic; may include the following:
  - **Diagrams:** pictures with labels
  - **Maps:** pictures that show where something is or how to get from one place to another place
  - **Graphs/Charts:** pictures that help readers compare pieces of information
  - **Timeline:** shows the important events about a topic over a period of time
- **Text Features:** ways the author makes words stand out; may include the following:
  - **Headings:** type—usually larger, darker, or both—at the beginning of a new section
  - **Captions:** words or sentences that explain a picture
  - **Sizes/Colors:** authors use different sizes and colors to help readers see what is most important
- **Main Idea:** what the book is mostly about
- **Details:** pieces of information that tell more about the main idea or topic
- **Text Structure:** how the book is organized, such as by sequence of events, cause and effect, or compare and contrast
- **Fact:** a piece of information that is true and can be proved
- **Opinion:** a statement of what the author thinks or believes

Journeys Literature

STUDENT BOOK
All in the Family
Animals Building Homes
Basket Weaving
From Eggs to Frogs
The Goat in the Rug
Heroes Then and Now
How to Make a Kite
Jackie Robinson
Jellies
La Brea Tar Pits
Meet Norbert Wu
A Model Citizen
My Family
Now & Ben
Outdoor Adventures
Penguin Chick
Playground Fun
Schools Around the World
See Westburg by Bus!
Super Soil
Super Storms
Talk About Smart Animals!
Talking Tools
They Really Are GIANT!
Working in Space

TEACHER'S EDITION READ-ALOUD
Bats: Beastly or Beautiful?
City Life Is for the Birds
Godmothers and Goats
Don't Play Cards with a Dog in the Room!
Dr. Salk's Treasure
Epperson's Icicle
Floods: Dangerous Water
From Duckling to Duck
More Than a Best Friend
Nothing But a Quilt
One-Room Schoolhouse
Sharks on the Run!
Solving Problems with New Inventions
Whale of a Lesson
Wild Friends, Wow!

LEVELED READERS

All About Chile K
Along Came a Spider . . . J
Amazing Nests I
America's First Firefighters M
Animals at the Aquarium H
Antarctic Animals L
Art Is All Around You O
Baseball Firsts P
Bees at Work L
Being a Spider N
Ben Franklin, Founding Father Q
Birthdays Around the World J
Bongos, Maracas, and Xylophones I
Bottlenose Dolphins O
The Brooklyn Dodgers J
A Busy Beaver I
Busy Bees L
C-A-M-P! Camp! K
Clever Animals J
Composting N
Coral Reefs I
Creatures of the Deep O
A Day in San Juan M
Digging Up Dinosaurs! O
Dinosaur Fossils I
Everyday Hero I
Fall Harvest I
Firefighters in America M
Fitness and Training N
Folktales Around the World N

Friendship Rules! I
From Sheep to Sweater J
From Trails to Highways Q
From Typewriters to Computers K
Fun Pets H
Grow a Bean Plant! I
Growing Up in the Pond N
Guide Dog School J
Happy Birthday, Everyone J
How to Make a Family Tree N
How We Use Wool M
The International Space Station O
Lessons About Lightning N
Let It Rain! I
Let's Make Music! I
Life in Tide Pools K
The Lives of Ants O
The Loch Ness Monster I
Making a Newspaper M
Native American Folktales J
The Navajo P
One Room Schools I
Pet Rabbits I
Philadelphia, 1756 M
Poles Apart Q
Police in the Community I
Predicting the Weather P
Raising Funds J
Ready for Liftoff L
The Red Planet O
Rhythm Is Everywhere N

School in a Garden, A N
School Long Ago M
Secrets in the Sea O
Signs All Around Us M
Signs Are Everywhere J
A Snowy Day G
Speaking in Sign O
Special Tools J
Spread the Word N
Staying Healthy in Space L
Take a Trip to China L
Terra-Cotta Army P
Textiles from Around the World Q
The Three Sisters J
Tide Pools K
The Tie O
The Tools of Investigators M
Training a Dog M
A Trip Through Africa O
Trouble in Space M
Trouble on a Trip to the Moon M
Underground Homes N
Vegetables Around the World O
A Visit to the Andes O
Weaving K
Welcoming New Neighbors M
What Is in the Wind? L
What School Was Like Long Ago K
Who Is in Your Family? F
The Wind L
Wool M

Biography

SUPPORT THINKING

DISCUSSION STARTERS During whole-group and small-group discussion, use questions to spark conversation about genre characteristics.

- Who is this book about?
- What is/was [subject name] like?
- What important things happened to [subject name]?
- Where did [subject name] live?
- What did other people think about [subject name]?
- What is the author trying to tell readers about [subject name]?
- Why is it important to know about [subject name]'s life?
- How does the author organize this biography?
- What can you learn from [subject name]'s life?
- What questions do you still have about [subject name]?

COMPARING TEXTS After children have read and listened to several biographies, prompt them to compare selections and to recognize common characteristics. Use questions such as these:

- How are [subject name] and [subject name] the same?
- How is [title] the same as other biographies you have read? How is it different?
- Which person would you like to read more about? Explain.
- Of all the biographies you've read, which tells about the most interesting person? Explain.

Helen Keller, Student Book, Lesson 14

My Name Is Gabriela, Student Book, Lesson 18

Genre Characteristics

A biography is the true story of a real person's life.

Through repeated exposure to biographies, children should learn to notice common genre characteristics, though they will not be expected to use all the technical labels. Use friendly language to help them understand the following concepts:

- **Author's Purpose:** to inform; to show why this person's life is important
- **Characters:** the subject is the real person the biography is about; other characters are people in the subject's life
- **Setting:** the place where the subject lived, worked, or traveled
- **Important Events:** told in the order they happened
- **Facts and Opinions:** help readers understand how the author feels and why the subject's life is important
- **Narrative Structure:** events told in order as a story; may tell about all or just part of the person's life

Journeys Literature

STUDENT BOOK
The Dog That Dug for Dinosaurs
Helen Keller
My Name Is Gabriela
Wolfgang Mozart, Child Superstar

TEACHER'S EDITION READ-ALOUD
An Apple a Day
Tiger Woods: Superstar in Golf and Life

LEVELED READERS
The Adventures of Erik **O**
Alexander Graham Bell **M**
Anne Sullivan **J**
Beatrix Potter **K**
Inventor of the Telephone **M**
Jack Prelutsky **M**
The Life of Jack Prelutsky **M**
The Life of Langston Hughes **P**
The Mysterious Bone **L**
Sir Hans Sloane **O**
Sue Hendrickson **M**
Sue Hendrickson: Fossil Hunter **L**

110 • Teaching Genre: Biography

Teacher's Notes

Leveled Readers Database

Guided Reading Level	Title	Grade Pack	DRA Level	Lexile Level	Reading Recovery Level	Genre	Word Count
F	Who Is in Your Family?	2VR	10	250	10	Informational Text	229
G	Firedog!	2	12	460	11	Humorous Fiction	217
G	Grandma's Surprise	2	12	270	11	Realistic Fiction	220
G	Real Band, A	2	12	250	12	Realistic Fiction	183
G	Snowy Day, A	2	12	440	11	Informational Text	232
G	Winning Hit, The	2	12	170	12	Realistic Fiction	274
H	Animals at the Aquarium	2	14	350	13	Informational Text	259
H	Ben and Sooty	2	14	280	14	Realistic Fiction	152
H	Billy, the Pet Bird	2	14	370	14	Realistic Fiction	371
H	Caty the Caterpillar	2	14	300	13	Realistic Fiction	175
H	Cub Saves the Day	2	14	280	13	Humorous Fiction	156
H	Fun Pets	2VR	14	320	13	Informational Text	190
H	Giant Forest, The	2	14	490	13	Fantasy	269
H	Zoo Party	2	14	390	13	Humorous Fiction	271
I	Aldo and Abby	2	16	240	15	Humorous Fiction	235
I	Amazing Nests	2VR	16	630	16	Informational Text	270
I	Bongos, Maracas, and Xylophones	2VR	16	280	15	Informational Text	210
I	Brer Rabbit at the Well	2	16	510	15	Folktale	268
I	Busy Beaver, A	2	16	660	15	Informational Text	323
I	Camel's Hump	2	16	340	16	Folktale	274
I	Chipmunks Do What Chipmunks Do	2	16	280	16	Fantasy	138
I	Colors of Leaves, The	2	16	330	16	Fantasy	561
I	Coral Reefs	2VR	16	650	15	Informational Text	266
I	Dinosaur Fossils	2VR	16	660	16	Informational Text	370
I	Everyday Hero	2VR	16	600	16	Informational Text	249
I	Fall Harvest	2VR	16	150	16	Informational Text	179
I	Friendship Rules!	2VR	16	500	15	Informational Text	256
I	Grow a Bean Plant!	2VR	16	540	15	Informational Text	220
I	Kite Contest, The	2	16	360	16	Realistic Fiction	346
I	Let It Rain!	2VR	16	420	15	Informational Text	257

112 • Leveled Readers Database

ONLINE LEVELED READERS DATABASE

- Go to www.thinkcentral.com for the complete *Journeys* Online Leveled Readers Database.
- Search by grade, genre, title, or level.

Author's Purpose	Cause and Effect	Compare and Contrast	Conclusions	Fact and Opinion	Main Ideas and Details	Sequence of Events	Story Structure	Text and Graphic Features	Theme	Understanding Characters
●		●			●			●		
	●		●			●	●			●
			●			●				●
●		●				●	●			●
●	●	●		●	●					
	●					●	●		●	●
●		●		●	●			●		
	●	●	●			●			●	
	●	●				●				●
	●					●	●			●
	●		●			●	●		●	●
●		●		●	●					
		●				●	●		●	
	●	●	●			●	●			●
	●	●				●		●	●	●
●		●			●			●		
●		●			●			●		
●	●		●				●			●
●				●	●			●		
●	●		●			●	●		●	●
						●			●	●
●						●			●	●
●	●	●	●	●	●					
●			●		●			●		
●			●		●					
●	●				●					
●					●					
●						●		●		
	●	●				●	●		●	●
●	●	●	●		●					

Leveled Readers Database • 113

Leveled Readers Database

Guided Reading Level	Title	Grade Pack	DRA Level	Lexile Level	Reading Recovery Level	Genre	Word Count
I	Let's Make Music!	2 ●	16	180	15	Informational Text	185
I	Loch Ness Monster, The	2VR	16	630	16	Informational Text	362
I	One Room Schools	2VR	16	320	15	Informational Text	250
I	Our Library	2 ●	16	300	16	Realistic Fiction	320
I	Pet Rabbits	2VR	16	480	15	Informational Text	366
I	Police in the Community	2VR	16	530	15	Informational Text	225
I	Staying Healthy in Space	2 ●	16	560	16	Informational Text	291
I	Two Heroes	2 ●	16	310	16	Fantasy	282
J	Along Came a Spider . . .	2VR	18	440	18	Informational Text	257
J	Anne Sullivan	2 ●	18	420	18	Biography	255
J	Best Student, The	2 ◆	18	360	18	Humorous Fiction	390
J	Birthdays Around the World	2 ◆	18	510	18	Informational Text	375
J	Brooklyn Dodgers, The	2VR	18	570	18	Informational Text	323
J	Clever Animals	2VR	18	550	18	Informational Text	332
J	Community Garden, The	2 ▲	18	550	18	Realistic Fiction	419
J	Elena's Wish	2 ◆	18	370	18	Realistic Fiction	708
J	Favorite Fables	2 ●	18	430	18	Fable	668
J	Flora the Fly Saves the Spiders	2 ◆	18	250	18	Humorous Fiction	353
J	Fly to the Rescue!	2 ▲	18	300	18	Humorous Fiction	384
J	Foster's Famous Farm	2 ◆	18	410	18	Realistic Fiction	352
J	Foster's Farm	2 ▲	18	520	18	Realistic Fiction	323
J	From Sheep to Sweater	2 ●	18	520	18	Informational Text	266
J	Good Citizen	2 ▲	18	500	18	Humorous Fiction	372
J	Guide Dog School	2 ●	18	480	18	Informational Text	348
J	Happy Birthday, Everyone	2 ▲	18	540	18	Informational Text	339
J	Larry the Singing Chicken	2 ●	18	300	18	Fantasy	333
J	Luz and the Garden	2 ◆	18	420	18	Realistic Fiction	446
J	Native American Folktales	2VR	18	640	18	Informational Text	288
J	Penguins	2 ●	18	490	18	Narrative Nonfiction	311
J	Raising Funds	2VR	18	610	18	Informational Text	250

ONLINE LEVELED READERS DATABASE

- Go to www.thinkcentral.com for the complete *Journeys* Online Leveled Readers Database.
- Search by grade, genre, title, or level.

Author's Purpose	Cause and Effect	Compare and Contrast	Conclusions	Fact and Opinion	Main Ideas and Details	Sequence of Events	Story Structure	Text and Graphic Features	Theme	Understanding Characters
●		●			●			●		
●	●		●	●	●	●		●		
		●			●			●		
●	●		●				●		●	●
●					●					
●		●	●		●			●		
●			●	●				●		
			●	●		●	●		●	●
●			●		●					
●	●			●				●		
	●		●			●				●
●		●		●	●			●		
●		●			●	●		●		
●		●	●		●			●		
					●					●
	●		●			●	●		●	●
	●					●	●		●	●
●		●	●			●	●		●	●
●	●	●	●			●	●		●	●
●	●		●			●			●	●
						●	●		●	
●			●	●	●			●		
	●		●			●				●
●					●					
●		●		●				●		
	●	●	●			●	●		●	●
			●			●				●
●				●	●	●				
					●			●		
●	●		●		●			●		

Leveled Readers Database • **115**

Leveled Readers Database

Guided Reading Level	Title	Grade Pack	DRA Level	Lexile Level	Reading Recovery Level	Genre	Word Count
J	Rosa the Painter	2 ◆	18	300	18	Realistic Fiction	394
J	Signs Are Everywhere	2VR	18	380	18	Informational Text	276
J	Smiths and Their Animals, The	2 ◆	18	400	18	Humorous Fiction	468
J	Special Tools	2VR	18	500	18	Informational Text	266
J	Superheroes Save the Day	2 ◆	18	280	18	Fantasy	714
J	Superheroes to the Rescue	2 ▲	18	410	18	Fantasy	736
J	Three Sisters, The	2VR	18	480	18	Informational Text	313
J	Trick, The	2 ◆	18	330	18	Folktale	550
J	What Can Rosa Paint?	2 ▲	18	440	18	Realistic Fiction	383
K	All About Chile	2VR	20	550	18	Informational Text	271
K	Bake Sale, The	2 ▲	20	580	18	Realistic Fiction	605
K	Beatrix Potter	2 ●	20	390	18	Biography	314
K	C-A-M-P! Camp!	2CY	20	540	18	Informational Text	595
K	Every Kind of Wish	2 ▲	20	360	18	Realistic Fiction	664
K	Finding the Party	2 ▲	20	300	18	Humorous Fiction	613
K	From Typewriters to Computers	2VR	20	540	18	Informational Text	312
K	How Coyote Stole Fire	2 ▲	20	450	18	Folktale	544
K	How People Got Fire	2 ◆	20	390	18	Folktale	580
K	How the Leaves Got Their Colors	2 ▲	20	310	18	Fantasy	476
K	Jason and the Space Creature	2 ◆	20	330	18	Fantasy	643
K	Life in Tide Pools	2 ▲	20	560	18	Informational Text	383
K	Ms. Hawkins and the Bake Sale	2 ◆	20	530	18	Realistic Fiction	643
K	Pay Attention!	2 ▲	20	530	18	Humorous Fiction	458
K	Sam Finds the Party	2 ◆	20	270	18	Humorous Fiction	714
K	Smart Mouse, The	2 ◆	20	380	18	Folktale	597
K	Summer of Baseball Parks, The	2 ◆	20	460	18	Realistic Fiction	690
K	Take Me Out to the Ballpark	2 ▲	20	440	18	Realistic Fiction	711
K	Tide Pools	2 ◆	20	490	18	Informational Text	388
K	Weaving	2VR	20	510	18	Informational Text	256
K	What School Was Like Long Ago	2 ◆	20	410	18	Informational Text	499

116 • Leveled Readers Database

ONLINE LEVELED READERS DATABASE

- Go to www.thinkcentral.com for the complete *Journeys* Online Leveled Readers Database.
- Search by grade, genre, title, or level.

Author's Purpose	Cause and Effect	Compare and Contrast	Conclusions	Fact and Opinion	Main Ideas and Details	Sequence of Events	Story Structure	Text and Graphic Features	Theme	Understanding Characters
			●			●	●		●	●
●	●		●	●	●					
	●		●			●	●		●	●
●	●	●	●	●	●			●		
	●	●	●		●	●	●		●	●
	●	●	●		●	●	●		●	●
●		●			●	●		●		
	●					●	●		●	●
			●			●	●		●	●
●		●		●	●			●		●
	●	●	●			●	●		●	●
●			●		●			●		●
		●	●						●	●
	●		●	●		●	●		●	●
			●					●	●	●
●	●	●	●		●	●			●	●
●	●		●			●	●		●	●
●	●		●			●	●		●	●
●						●				●
	●	●	●		●			●	●	●
●			●		●					
	●	●	●			●	●		●	●
	●		●			●	●		●	●
			●					●	●	●
●	●		●			●				●
●			●			●				●
●			●			●				●
●			●	●		●			●	
			●			●		●	●	
●			●	●		●		●		

Leveled Readers Database • 117

Leveled Readers Database

Guided Reading Level	Title	Grade Pack	DRA Level	Lexile Level	Reading Recovery Level	Genre	Word Count
L	Annie's Pictures	2 ■	24	390	20	Realistic Fiction	460
L	Antarctic Animals	2VR	24	660	20	Informational Text	328
L	Bees at Work	2 ◆	24	600	20	Informational Text	456
L	Busy Bees	2 ▲	24	640	20	Informational Text	417
L	Lucy and Billy	2 ▲	24	410	20	Realistic Fiction	317
L	Mouse and Crocodile	2 ▲	24	520	20	Folktale	573
L	Mysterious Bone, The	2 ●	24	460	20	Biography	320
L	Mysterious Superhero, The	2 ■	24	620	20	Fantasy	1,104
L	Planet Zogo	2 ▲	24	430	20	Fantasy	663
L	Rabbit's Garden	2 ◆	24	410	20	Fantasy	661
L	Rabbit's Garden Troubles	2 ▲	24	470	20	Fantasy	652
L	Ready for Liftoff	2VR	24	670	20	Informational Text	294
L	Sue Hendrickson: Fossil Hunter	2 ◆	24	690	20	Biography	671
L	Take a Trip to China	2VR	24	570	20	Informational Text	301
L	Too Many Signs!	2 ■	24	450	20	Humorous Fiction	978
L	What Is in the Wind?	2 ▲	24	610	20	Informational Text	472
L	Where Is Gus-Gus?	2 ■	24	470	20	Realistic Fiction	861
L	Wind, The	2 ◆	24	540	20	Informational Text	445
M	Alexander Graham Bell	2 ▲	28	590	20	Biography	416
M	America's First Firefighters	2 ▲	28	630	20	Informational Text	619
M	Coyote and the Rabbit	2 ▲	28	500	20	Folktale	1,018
M	Day in San Juan, A	2CY	28	450	20	Informational Text	621
M	Firefighters in America	2 ◆	28	500	20	Informational Text	619
M	How We Use Wool	2 ◆	28	620	20	Informational Text	654
M	Inventor of the Telephone	2 ◆	28	460	20	Biography	448
M	Jack Prelutsky	2 ◆	28	500	20	Biography	690
M	Life of Jack Prelutsky, The	2 ▲	28	540	20	Biography	632
M	Making a Newspaper	2 ●	28	610	20	Informational Text	317
M	New Field, The	2 ■	28	660	20	Realistic Fiction	945
M	Pet That Fits, A	2 ■	28	600	20	Realistic Fiction	404

ONLINE LEVELED READERS DATABASE

- Go to www.thinkcentral.com for the complete *Journeys* Online Leveled Readers Database.
- Search by grade, genre, title, or level.

Author's Purpose	Cause and Effect	Compare and Contrast	Conclusions	Fact and Opinion	Main Ideas and Details	Sequence of Events	Story Structure	Text and Graphic Features	Theme	Understanding Characters
●						●	●		●	●
●		●			●			●		
●			●	●	●			●		
●			●	●	●			●		
	●	●				●				●
●	●		●			●	●		●	●
●			●	●	●	●		●		
		●	●				●		●	●
	●						●			●
●	●	●	●			●	●		●	●
●	●	●	●			●	●			●
				●	●			●		
	●			●	●			●		
●				●			●	●		
	●	●				●	●	●	●	●
●	●	●		●						
	●			●				●	●	●
●	●	●		●	●					
●		●	●		●	●				
●			●		●					
	●					●	●		●	●
●			●		●		●			
●			●		●					
		●	●	●				●		
●			●	●			●			●
●			●	●			●			●
●			●				●	●		
	●			●		●	●			●
	●		●							●

Leveled Readers Database • 119

Leveled Readers Database

Guided Reading Level	Title	Grade Pack	DRA Level	Lexile Level	Reading Recovery Level	Genre	Word Count
M	Philadelphia, 1756	2VR	28	490	20	Informational Text	273
M	School Long Ago	2 ▲	28	330	20	Informational Text	430
M	Signs All Around Us	2CY	28	660	20	Informational Text	900
M	Sue Hendrickson	2 ▲	28	680	20	Biography	632
M	Tools of Investigators, The	2CY	28	500	20	Informational Text	575
M	Town Auction, The	2 ■	28	650	20	Realistic Fiction	866
M	Training a Dog	2CY	28	650	20	Informational Text	591
M	Trouble in Space	2 ▲	28	790	20	Informational Text	725
M	Trouble on a Trip to the Moon	2 ◆	28	690	20	Informational Text	723
M	Welcoming New Neighbors	2CY	28	750	20	Informational Text	916
M	Well-Trained Dog, A	2 ■	28	530	20	Humorous Fiction	797
M	Wool	2 ▲	28	750	20	Informational Text	660
N	Bee's Beautiful Garden	2 ■	34	660	22	Fantasy	720
N	Being a Spider	2CY	30	650	22	Informational Text	694
N	Composting	2CY	30	690	22	Informational Text	755
N	E-Mails from the Teacher	2 ■	30	610	22	Humorous Fiction	915
N	Ferdinand Saves the Day	2 ■	34	520	22	Humorous Fiction	889
N	Fitness and Training	2CY	30	640	22	Informational Text	667
N	Folktales Around the World	2CY	30	700	22	Informational Text	757
N	Groundhog's New Home	2 ■	34	740	22	Folktale	1,076
N	Growing Up in the Pond	2CY	30	580	22	Informational Text	799
N	How to Make a Family Tree	2 ■	30	530	22	Informational Text	928
N	Katy's Inventions	2 ■	30	390	22	Fantasy	804
N	Lessons About Lightning	2 ■	34	610	22	Informational Text	850
N	Rhythm Is Everywhere	2CY	30	680	22	Informational Text	532
N	Sand Castle Contest	2 ■	30	460	22	Realistic Fiction	949
N	School in a Garden, A	2 ■	34	600	22	Informational Text	887
N	Spread the Word	2CY	30	780	22	Informational Text	693
N	Uncle Rabbit	2 ■	34	630	22	Folktale	891
N	Underground Homes	2CY	30	760	22	Informational Text	800

ONLINE LEVELED READERS DATABASE

- Go to www.thinkcentral.com for the complete *Journeys* Online Leveled Readers Database.
- Search by grade, genre, title, or level.

Author's Purpose	Cause and Effect	Compare and Contrast	Conclusions	Fact and Opinion	Main Ideas and Details	Sequence of Events	Story Structure	Text and Graphic Features	Theme	Understanding Characters
●		●	●							
●		●			●			●		
●	●		●	●				●		
●			●	●	●			●		
	●		●	●						
	●					●	●			●
●			●		●			●		
●	●		●			●		●		
●	●		●		●	●		●		
●	●			●		●		●		
●	●		●		●		●		●	●
●		●	●							
	●					●	●			●
●		●		●				●		
	●			●	●			●		
	●					●	●			●
	●								●	
●		●		●	●			●		
●			●					●		
						●	●		●	●
		●	●		●					
●						●	●			
	●		●			●	●			●
●	●		●	●	●			●		●
●			●	●				●		
		●				●	●		●	●
●			●		●	●				
●			●		●	●				
	●		●			●	●		●	●
●		●		●	●					

Leveled Readers Database • **121**

Leveled Readers Database

Guided Reading Level	Title	Grade Pack	DRA Level	Lexile Level	Reading Recovery Level	Genre	Word Count
O	Adventures of Erik, The	2 ■	38	670	24	Biography	956
O	Art Is All Around You	2CY	38	700	24	Informational Text	720
O	Bottlenose Dolphins	2 ■	38	630	24	Informational Text	964
O	Creatures of the Deep	2CY	38	630	24	Informational Text	842
O	Cross-Country Cousins	2 ■	38	690	24	Realistic Fiction	919
O	Digging Up Dinosaurs!	2CY	38	700	24	Informational Text	848
O	Going to the South Pole	2 ◆	38	490	24	Narrative Nonfiction	843
O	International Space Station, The	2CY	38	930	24	Informational Text	798
O	Lives of Ants, The	2 ■	38	750	24	Informational Text	1,054
O	Red Planet, The	2 ■	38	760	24	Informational Text	765
O	Secrets in the Sea	2CY	38	780	24	Informational Text	798
O	Sir Hans Sloane	2 ■	38	600	24	Biography	765
O	Speaking in Sign	2CY	38	830	24	Informational Text	778
O	Thousand Words, A	2 ■	38	430	24	Realistic Fiction	689
O	Tie, The	2CY	38	750	24	Informational Text	819
O	Trip Through Africa, A	2CY	38	770	24	Informational Text	971
O	Vegetables Around the World	2CY	38	650	24	Informational Text	709
O	Visit to the Andes, A	2CY	38	730	24	Informational Text	865
P	Baseball Firsts	2CY	38	740	24	Informational Text	1,059
P	Exploring Antarctica	2 ▲	38	500	24	Narrative Nonfiction	745
P	Life of Langston Hughes, The	2 ■	38	660	24	Biography	1,003
P	McMurdo Station	2 ■	38	700	24	Narrative Nonfiction	861
P	Navajo, The	2CY	38	800	24	Informational Text	830
P	Predicting the Weather	2CY	38	800	24	Informational Text	857
P	Terra-Cotta Army	2CY	38	790	24	Informational Text	920
P	Wali Dad's Gifts	2 ■	38	660	24	Folktale	1,003
Q	Ben Franklin, Founding Father	2CY	40	720	26	Informational Text	1,030
Q	From Trails to Highways	2 ■	40	830	26	Informational Text	919
Q	Poles Apart	2CY	40	710	26	Informational Text	978
Q	Textiles from Around the World	2 ■	40	880	26	Informational Text	851

ONLINE LEVELED READERS DATABASE

- Go to www.thinkcentral.com for the complete *Journeys* Online Leveled Readers Database.
- Search by grade, genre, title, or level.

Author's Purpose	Cause and Effect	Compare and Contrast	Conclusions	Fact and Opinion	Main Ideas and Details	Sequence of Events	Story Structure	Text and Graphic Features	Theme	Understanding Characters
●	●		●	●	●			●		
		●			●					
●		●		●	●			●		
		●		●				●		
●	●	●	●			●	●		●	●
●	●			●	●			●		
●					●	●		●		
		●				●				
●	●	●			●			●		
●		●	●		●	●		●		
		●		●	●			●		
●	●			●	●	●		●		
●					●			●		
	●		●			●	●		●	●
	●					●		●		
●	●				●			●		
●		●			●			●		
●				●				●		
●	●			●		●		●		
●					●			●		
●			●	●	●	●		●		●
●			●		●					
	●					●				
●				●	●					
				●		●				
●	●			●			●		●	●
	●			●						
●		●			●	●		●		
		●		●	●					
●		●	●	●	●			●		

Leveled Readers Database • 123

Literature Discussion

For small-group literature discussion, use the suggested trade book titles on the pages that follow, or select age-appropriate texts from your library or classroom collection.

Engage children in discussions to build understanding of the text, deepen comprehension, and foster children's confidence in talking about what they read. Encourage children to share their ideas about the text and also to build upon one another's ideas.

 Classic

 Science

 Social Studies

 Music

 Math

 Art

Suggested Trade Book Titles

BIOGRAPHY

Ada, Alma Flor and F. Isabel Campoy. *Smiles: Pablo Picasso, Gabriela Mistral, Benito Juarez.* Readers learn about the lives of three notable Hispanic artists and leaders. Santillana, 2000 (32p).

Brown, Monica. *My Name Is Celia: The Life of Celia Cruz.* This bilingual, musical biography of Cuban-born Celia Cruz follows her as she makes her way from Havana, Cuba, to become an internationally known salsa queen. Rising Moon, 2004 (32p).

Ehrhardt, Karen. *This Jazz Man.* Nine well-known jazz musicians are introduced in text set to the rhythm of the traditional song "This Old Man." Harcourt, 2006 (32p).

Hoena, B. A. *Langston Hughes: Great American Writer.* This biography introduces the life of African American writer Langston Hughes, who shared his feelings about racism through his works. Capstone, 2005 (32p).

FABLE

Blair, Eric. *The Crow and the Pitcher: A Retelling of Aesop's Fable.* In this classic tale, Crow uses his brain to figure out how to get a refreshing sip of water. **Available in Spanish as** *El cuervo y la jarra: Versión de la fábula de Esopo.* Picture Window Books, 2004 (24p).

Brett, Jan. *Town Mouse, Country Mouse.* In this stylized retelling of the classic fable, two pairs of mice learn a familiar lesson: There is no place like home. G.P. Putnam's Sons, 1994 (32p).

Morpurgo, Michael. *The McElderry Book of Aesop's Fables.* This collection has 21 beautifully retold and illustrated tales from Aesop. Margaret K. McElderry, 2005 (96p).

Watts, Bernadette. *The Lion and the Mouse.* This retelling of Aesop's fable shows the meaning of true friendship. North-South, 2000 (24p).

FAIRY TALE

Appleby, Ellen. *The Three Billy-Goats Gruff.* Three goats make their way across a bridge and outsmart a tricky troll on the way. Scholastic Paperbacks, 1991 (32p).

dePaola, Tomie. *Little Grunt and the Big Egg: A Prehistoric Fairy Tale.* Little Grunt is surprised when out of his special egg hatches a lively baby dinosaur. Puffin, 2008 (24p).

Marshall, James. *Goldilocks and the Three Bears.* Goldilocks makes herself at home in the bears' house, but the bears are not pleased with what they find when they return home. Dial, 1988 (32p).

Marshall, James. *Red Riding Hood.* Red Riding Hood is reminded of why she shouldn't talk to strangers when she meets a seemingly charming wolf on her way to Grandma's house. Picture Puffins, 1993 (32p).

FANTASY

Albee, Sarah. *My New Pet Is the Greatest.* When Sam brings home a baby dinosaur, his new pet's size and silly antics create unusual problems for his family. Random House, 2003 (32p).

Appelt, Kathi. *Bat Jamboree.* Each year, at an abandoned outdoor theater, fifty-five bats perform in a musical and theatrical revue, building up to the grand finale. HarperTrophy, 1998 (32p).

Bechtold, Lisze. *Buster: The Very Shy Dog.* In three stories, Buster the dog overcomes his shyness, discovers his special talent, and helps Phoebe find the garbage bandits. Houghton Mifflin, 2001 (48p).

Brown, Marc. *Arthur Writes a Story.* Arthur's homework assignment is to write a story, but he keeps changing his idea of what to write. **Available in Spanish as** *Arturo escribe un cuento.* Little, Brown, 1998 (32p).

Brown, Marc. *D. W. Rides Again!* When D. W. receives her first tricycle, her older brother, Arthur, teaches her the rules of riding in the community. Little, Brown, 1996 (32p).

Burton, Virginia Lee. *The Little House.* A little house in the country finds that, over time, a city has grown up around her. **Available in Spanish as** *La casita.* Houghton, 1943 (44p).

Ehlert, Lois. *Leaf Man.* In creative collages, this story shows how scattered leaves can take imaginative shapes. Harcourt, 2005 (40p).

Ernest, Lisa Campbell. *Goldilocks Returns.* Fifty years later, Goldilocks, now known as Goldi, returns to the three bears' cottage because she has some issues to resolve. Aladdin, 2003 (40p).

Frasier, Debra. *A Birthday Cake Is No Ordinary Cake.* How time passes between one birthday and the next is explained to the reader by means of a lyrical recipe using changes in the natural world. Harcourt, 2006 (40p).

Forward, Toby. *The Wolf's Story: What Really Happened to Little Red Riding Hood.* The wolf tells his side of the story of Little Red Riding Hood, declaring that he was not trying to eat Grandma, but instead was trying to help her. Candlewick, 2005 (32p).

Howard, Arthur. *Cosmo Zooms.* Cosmo the dog discovers a special talent when he accidentally takes a nap on a skateboard. Harcourt, 2003 (32p).

Kavanagh, Peter. *I Love My Mama.* Readers follow along as a mother and her baby elephant splash in the water, soak up the sun, and lie in the grass. Simon & Schuster, 2003 (32p).

Keller, Laurie. *The Scrambled States of America.* The states are bored with where they are on the map and decide to trade places for a while. Henry Holt, 2002 (40p).

Komaiko, Leah. *Just My Dad & Me.* When a young girl's day doesn't turn out how she had hoped, she imagines herself alone with fish that take on familiar appearances. HarperTrophy, 1999 (32p).

Lithgow, John. *Micawber.* Micawber, a squirrel fascinated by art, accompanies an art student and uses her supplies to make his own paintings. Simon & Schuster, 2002 (40p).

London, Jonathan. *Froggy Plays Soccer.* Froggy is very excited because his Dream Team is playing for the city soccer championship, but he forgets a rule and almost costs the team the game. **Available in Spanish as** *Froggy juega al fútbol.* Viking, 1999 (32p).

Mayer, Mercer. *Just Me and My Puppy.* A child trades his baseball mitt for a puppy and learns the importance of playtime and being responsible in this comical story. Golden, 1998 (24p).

McCloskey, Robert. *Lentil.* In this classic story, a boy named Lentil brings his entire community together by joyfully playing his harmonica. Puffin, 1978 (62p).

McKee, David. *Elmer.* Elmer, a colorful elephant, is different from the other elephants of the jungle. He decides to blend in to look like the others. HarperCollins, 1989 (32p).

Meister, Cari. *Tiny's Bath.* Tiny is a big dog that loves to dig, and when he needs a bath, his owner has trouble finding a place to bathe him. Puffin, 1999 (32p).

Most, Bernard. *The Cow That Went OINK.* A cow that oinks and a pig that moos are teased by the other barnyard animals. The cow and the pig get the last laugh when each teaches the other a new sound. **Available in Spanish as** *La vaca que decía OINK.* Harcourt, 2003 (40p).

Rosenthal, Marc. *Phooey!* A boy, angry that his town is so dull, kicks an empty can and sets off a chain reaction of exciting events. HarperCollins/Cotler, 2007 (40p).

Seuss, Dr. *I Can Read with My Eyes Shut!* The Cat in the Hat shows Young Cat the fun he can get out of reading. **Available in Spanish as** *¡Yo puedo leer con los ojos cerrados!* Random House, 1978 (48p).

Steinberg, Laya. *Thesaurus Rex.* Thesaurus Rex, a lovable dinosaur, introduces children to synonyms in this rhyming text that takes him through his day. Barefoot, 2003 (24p).

Wells, Rosemary. *Bunny Cakes.* Max makes an earthworm cake and helps Ruby with her angel surprise cake for their Grandma's birthday. Max uses creative thinking to solve a problem with Ruby's shopping list. Puffin, 2000 (32p).

Wheeler, Lisa. *Farmer Dale's Red Pickup Truck.* Farmer Dale offers rides to animals he meets on his way to town in his rickety old pickup truck. Harcourt, 2006 (40p).

Yee, Wong Herbert. *Upstairs Mouse, Downstairs Mole.* Neighbors Mouse and Mole have their differences, but they learn that cooperation and compromise lead to friendship and fun. Houghton, 2005 (48p).

FOLKTALE

Chamberlin, Mary and Rich. *Mama Panya's Pancakes: A Village Tale from Kenya.* Mama Panya is making pancakes for dinner. Her son, Adika, is very excited and decides to invite all of their friends to dinner. Barefoot, 2006 (40p).

Forest, Heather. *Stone Soup.* Arriving at a village, two hungry travelers make a magical soup from a stone, and the villagers learn that the main ingredient is sharing. August House, 1998 (32p).

Lowell, Susan. *The Bootmaker and the Elves.* This retelling of the traditional folktale has a Western setting. Scholastic, 1997 (32p).

Literature Discussion

Mosel, Arlene. *Tikki Tikki Tembo.* Two brothers with very different names learn why it is important to listen. The boys' parents learn a lesson about naming their children. **Available in Spanish as *Tiki Tiki Tembo.*** Puffin, 1997 (32p).

Ziefert, Harriet. *The Cow in the House.* A young man lives in a house that he thinks is too noisy. He decides to go to a wise man for advice. Puffin, 1997 (32p).

INFORMATIONAL TEXT

Adamson, Heather. *A Day in the Life of a Farmer.* Readers learn that farmers begin their days at 5:00 A.M. and work until dinnertime. Capstone, 2000 (24p).

Adamson, Heather. *A Day in the Life of a Firefighter.* What do firefighters do all day? This book teaches readers how firefighters work around the clock to make communities safer. Capstone, 2000 (24p).

Adamson, Heather. *In My World.* Simple text and photographs introduce community concepts. Capstone, 2006 (24p).

Adamson, Heather. *Let's Play Soccer!* Simple text and photographs present the skills, equipment, and safety concerns of playing soccer. Capstone, 2006 (24p).

Asch, Frank. *The Sun Is My Favorite Star.* A child follows the sun throughout the day and discovers everything it can do. Harcourt, 2000 (32p).

Aylmore, Angela. *Plucking (Making Music).* Let's make music! Readers are encouraged to make music creatively in this vibrant book that explores various instruments and how to play them. Steck-Vaughn, 2006 (24p).

Barraclough, Sue. *Animals in the Wild (Animal Worlds).* This enriching look at various wildlife creatures explores the differences between the animals, including habitats, sounds, and movements. Raintree, 2005 (24p).

Barraclough, Sue. *Bees (Creepy Creatures).* In this colorful book, readers learn how bees eat, grow, and reproduce. Raintree, 2005 (24p).

Bernard, Robin. *A Tree for All Seasons.* This book examines the changes that occur in a sugar maple tree as the seasons progress. National Geographic, 2001 (16p).

Blackstone, Margaret. *This Is Soccer.* This basic introduction to the game of soccer covers its equipment, players, and plays. It also shows a game in progress. Henry Holt, 1999 (32p).

Bridges, Sarah. *I Drive a Fire Engine.* Follow Jackson the firefighter and his peers as they work together to put out fires. Picture Window, 2006 (24p).

Burleigh, Robert. *Hoops.* Poetic text and illustrations express the energy of the game of basketball. Harcourt, 2001 (32p).

Cleary, Brian P. *To Root, to Toot, to Parachute: What Is a Verb?* In this entertaining introduction to grammar, rhyming text and illustrations of comical cats present many examples of verbs. Carolrhoda, 2001 (32p).

Davis, Gary W. *From Rock to Fireworks (Changes).* This start-to-finish description shows the process of making fireworks, from mining the minerals to manufacturing the shells. Scholastic, 1998 (32p).

Demarest, Chris L. *Hotshots!* Rhyming text tells about the equipment and work of a team of firefighters as they battle a brushfire caused by a spark from a passing train. Margaret K. McElderry, 2003 (48p).

Dunphy, Madeleine. *Here Is the Tropical Rain Forest.* Cumulative text presents the animals and plants of the tropical rain forest, including their relationships with one another and their environment. Web of Life, 2006 (32p).

Frost, Helen. *The Grain Group.* Simple text and photographs explain foods that are part of the grain group and their nutritional importance. Pebble, 2000 (24p).

Gibbons, Gail. *The Art Box.* What will you find in an art box? Large illustrations show the tools that artists use to express themselves. Holiday House, 1998 (32p).

Gibbons, Gail. *Bicycle Book.* Readers learn all about bicycles, including history, safety, parts, and the variety of bikes that exist. Holiday House, 1999 (30p).

Gibbons, Gail. *Check It Out!: The Book About Libraries.* This book discusses what is found in a library and how different libraries serve their communities. Harcourt, 1988 (32p).

Gibbons, Gail. *Ducks!* Readers are informed about the wide variety of ducks that exist and how they communicate, feed, build nests, and raise ducklings. Holiday House, 2001 (32p).

Jackson, Abby. *Making Money.* Simple text and photographs tell why we have money, what happens to old money, and how new money is made. Yellow Umbrella, 2004 (20p).

Jango-Cohen, Judith. *Mount Rushmore.* This book describes the meaning, history, and creation of the stone monument to four American presidents carved into Mount Rushmore, South Dakota. Lerner, 2003 (32p).

Kalan, Robert. *Rain.* Brief text and illustrations describe a rainstorm. HarperCollins, 1991 (32p).

Keller, Kristin Thoennes. *From Milk to Ice Cream.* This introduction to the basic concepts of food production, distribution, and consumption traces the production of ice cream from milk to the finished product. Capstone, 2005 (24p).

126 • Literature Discussion

Leedy, Loreen. *Look at My Book: How Kids Can Write & Illustrate Terrific Books.* Ideas and simple directions are provided for writing, illustrating, designing, and binding books. Holiday House, 2005 (32p).

Lindeen, Carol K. *Life in a Rain Forest.* Simple text and photographs introduce the rain forest biome, including the environment, plants, and animals. Capstone, 2004 (24p).

Micucci, Charles. *The Life and Times of the Peanut.* The history and statistics of peanuts are introduced, as well as how they are grown and harvested and how peanut butter is made. Houghton Mifflin, 2000 (32p).

Miller, Heather. *Artist.* Readers learn what it is like to be an artist—from materials to workspaces—and about the different art professions that exist. **Available in Spanish as *Artista.*** Heinemann, 2003 (24p).

Morrison, Gordon. *Nature in the Neighborhood.* Readers learn how plants and animals in a neighborhood undergo changes throughout the seasons. Houghton/Lorraine, 2008 (32p).

Nelson, Robin. *From Flower to Honey.* This book describes how honey is made and sold, from bees drinking nectar from flowers to honey being processed by a beekeeper. Lerner, 2002 (24p).

Nelson, Robin. *From Peanut to Peanut Butter.* This is a brief introduction to the process by which peanuts are made into peanut butter. Lerner, 2003 (24p).

Pancella, Peggy. *Small Town (Neighborhood Walk).* Readers tour a small town and learn about workplaces, schools, transportation, and professions. Heinemann, 2005 (32p).

Preszler, June. *Bats (World of Mammals).* This brief introduction to bats discusses their characteristics, habitat, food, offspring, and the dangers they face. Bridgestone, 2006 (24p).

Rotner, Shelley and Sheila Kelly, Ed.D. *What Can You Do?: A Book About Discovering What You Do Well.* Different talents that make children unique—from skiing to spelling—are explored. Millbrook, 2001 (24p).

Rustad, Martha E. H. *Today Is Sunny.* Simple text and photographs present weather information, clothing choices, and activities for a sunny day. Capstone, 2006 (24p).

Sayre, April Pulley. *The Bumblebee Queen.* The queen of the hive has a lot of work to do! Join her as she leads her colony through the seasons of the year. Charlesbridge, 2006 (32p).

Sayre, April Pulley. *Good Morning, Africa! (Our Amazing Continents).* If you woke up in Africa, what might you see? Find out in this adventurous exploration of wildlife reserves, natural resources, and African cities. Millbrook, 2003 (32p).

Schmid, Eleonore. *The Living Earth.* Students learn how fragile Earth's ecosystem is and how important it is to nourish soil for harvests. North-South, 2000 (32p).

Suen, Anastasia. *The Story of Figure Skating.* Readers explore the history of figure skating in this fascinating book, which includes references to popular skaters from around the world. Rigby, 2001 (24p).

Suen, Anastasia. *The Story of Soccer.* Using simple text, the author describes the evolution of soccer throughout history, including current trends and famous soccer players. Rigby, 2001 (24p).

Thomas, Isabel. *Sculpting (Action Art).* Readers are introduced to sculpting techniques, materials, and processes. Heinemann, 2005 (24p).

Trumbauer, Lisa. *Living in a Small Town.* Simple text and photos describe life in small towns. Capstone, 2005 (24p).

Woelfle, Gretchen. *Animal Families, Animal Friends.* This book discusses animal parents, families, and communities and shows how groups of animals work together. NorthWord, 2005 (32p).

POETRY

Adoff, Arnold. *Street Music: City Poems.* The sights and sounds of life in a big city are shown through fifteen poems. HarperCollins, 1995 (32p).

Goldberg, Dana (editor). *On My Block: Stories and Paintings by Fifteen Artists.* Fifteen artists share and depict a place special to them, such as a rooftop, garden, or bottom bunk. Children's Book Press, 2007 (32p).

Greenfield, Eloise. *Under the Sunday Tree.* Life in the Bahamas is vividly described through poems and paintings. HarperTrophy, 1991 (48p).

Johnston, Tony. *Desert Song.* From dusk to daybreak, the desert abounds with life. Nocturnal animals such as bats, coyotes, and snakes venture out to find food in this lush and fragile wilderness. Gibbs Smith, 2000 (32p).

Larios, Julie. *Yellow Elephant: A Bright Bestiary.* Poems that explore familiar animals in extraordinary colors—from blue turtles to purple puppies—encourage readers to see the world in new ways. Harcourt, 2006 (32p).

Melmed, Laura Krauss. *New York, New York!: The Big Apple from A to Z.* Rhyming verse is paired with detailed paintings in this city ABC book. HarperCollins, 2005 (48p).

REALISTIC FICTION

Buckley, Helen E. *Grandfather and I.* A child considers how Grandfather is the perfect person to spend time with because he is never in a hurry. HarperTrophy, 2000 (24p).

Suggested Trade Book Titles • **127**

Literature Discussion

Cox, Judy. *My Family Plays Music.* A musically talented family celebrates by playing a variety of instruments. Holiday House, 2003 (32p).

Cutler, Jane. *Common Sense and Fowls.* The neighbors want Mrs. Krnc to stop feeding the pigeons, but Rachel, her friend Brian, and her great-uncle help the neighbors communicate and work it out. Farrar, 2005 (136p).

Daly, Niki. *Ruby Sings the Blues.* Ruby's loud singing bothers the neighbors, until two of them—a saxophone player and jazz singer—teach Ruby about volume control. Bloomsbury, 2005 (32p).

Falwell, Cathryn. *Butterflies for Kiri.* Kiri, a Japanese American girl who loves to draw and paint, tries to use the origami set she received for her birthday. Lee & Low, 2003 (32p).

Goodall, Jane. *Dr. White.* A small white dog visits children who are critically ill in the hospital and helps them recover. North-South, 2003 (36p).

Granowsky, Alvin. *At the Park (My World).* Spending a day at the park with their dog, a father and son have fun running, playing, and seeing many interesting sights. Copper Beech, 2001 (24p).

Grejniec, Michael. *What Do You Like?* Children learn that they often like the same things, but they enjoy them in different ways. **Available in Spanish as** *¿Qué te gusta?* North-South, 1995 (32p).

Guest, Elissa Haden. *Iris and Walter and the Substitute Teacher.* Iris's grandfather comes to her school as a substitute teacher. She has a hard time sharing him with the other students and becomes jealous. Harcourt, 2006 (44p).

Krebs, Laurie. *Off We Go to Mexico!: An Adventure in the Sun.* Take an exciting journey to Mexico in this colorful, rhyming story. Barefoot, 2006 (32p).

Maccarone, Grace. *I See a Leaf.* Walking to school in autumn, a group of students find fallen leaves to give to their teacher. Cartwheel, 2002 (32p).

Pfeffer, Wendy. *Marta's Magnets.* Marta has a magnet collection that her sister Rosa considers junk, but the magnets help Marta make friends in her new home and help her retrieve a key for Rosa's friend. Silver Burdett, 1995 (32p).

Rylant, Cynthia. *The Relatives Came.* Relatives from Virginia come to visit a family, and everyone has a fabulous time. Aladdin, 1993 (32p).

Schubert, Leda. *Here Comes Darrell.* Darrell is always willing to help his Vermont neighbors. When his own barn roof needs fixing, all the neighbors he has helped over the years pitch in to repair it. Houghton, 2005 (32p).

Spinelli, Eileen. *Heat Wave.* It's hot in Lumberville, and during the day the residents have their own way of dealing with the heat, but late at night they all gather along the riverbank with their pillows to try to get some sleep—and dream of rain. Harcourt, 2007 (32p).

Wells, Rosemary. *McDuff Moves In.* A little white dog that nobody wants finds just the right home—and a name. **Available in Spanish as** *McDuff encuentra un hogar.* Hyperion, 2005 (32p).

Williams, Vera B. *Something Special for Me.* Rosa, Mama, and Grandma fill a money jar with coins, saving to buy a treat. When it is Rosa's birthday, she chooses a present they can all enjoy. **Available in Spanish as** *Algo especial para mí.* HarperTrophy, 1986 (32p).

Wing, Natasha. *Jalapeño Bagels.* It is International Day at school, and Pablo decides to share something with his classmates that combines the cultures of both his parents. Atheneum, 1996 (32p).

Wong, Janet S. *Apple Pie 4th of July.* A Chinese American child thinks that the food her parents are preparing to sell on the Fourth of July will go uneaten. Harcourt, 2006 (40p).

Professional Bibliography

Barrentine, Shelley. "Engaging with reading through interactive read-alouds." *The Reading Teacher, 50(1):* 36–43.

Clay, Marie M. *Becoming Literate: The Construction of Inner Control.* Heinemann, 1991.

Clay, Marie M. *Change Over Time in Children's Literacy Development.* Heinemann, 2001.

Fountas, Irene. C. and G. S. Pinnell. *Guided Reading: Good First Teaching for All Children.* Heinemann, 1996.

Fountas, Irene C. and G. S. Pinnell. *Guiding Readers and Writers: Teaching Comprehension, Genre, and Content Literacy.* Heinemann, 2001.

Fountas, Irene C. and G. S. Pinnell. *Leveled Books, K–8: Matching Texts to Readers for Effective Teaching.* Heinemann, 2005.

Fountas, Irene C. and G. S. Pinnell. *Teaching for Comprehending and Fluency: Thinking, Talking, and Writing About Reading, K–8.* Heinemann, 2006.

Holdaway, Don. *The Foundations of Literacy.* Ashton Scholastic, 1979 (also Heinemann).

Pinnell, Gay Su and Irene C. Fountas. *The Continuum of Literacy Learning, Grades K–8: Behaviors and Understandings to Notice, Teach, and Support.* Heinemann, 2007.

Teacher's Notes